OPENING THE BOX

A Healer's Journey

David Robinson

authorHOUSE®

AuthorHouse™ UK Ltd.
500 Avebury Boulevard
Central Milton Keynes, MK9 2BE
www.authorhouse.co.uk
Phone: 08001974150

First published by AuthorHouse 6/5/2009

ISBN: 978-1-4389-5525-4 (sc)

This book is printed on acid-free paper.

Contents

Poetry

Dedication

This book is dedicated to my fellow travellers;
>   to those whom I have loved and still love,
>   to those with whom I have shared and still share,
>   to those I have carried and now carry me,
>   to those for whom I have opened a door for I stand in their light

Most of all, this book is dedicated to Marion, my wife and companion on this journey. She has shared my dreams and my visions and without her, we could not have accomplished so much. Whilst I have been up front doing what I have to do, she has worked tirelessly in the background, supporting and being a true advocate for spirit. Someone once asked me if I had met a truly spiritual person.
In her light, we all cast a great shadow.

David Robinson
Peacehaven,
Berriew,
Welshpool,
Powys.

Introduction

Some would say it was a mid-life crisis. It was. Most people have them. It is a wakeup call. It is part of their contract. It is in your contract and I know it was in mine. We all make contracts in our lives, physically, emotionally, mentally and spiritually, but more about that later.

It was during my thirty-seventh year in this present physical reality that my life took a different direction or perspective, or did a U-turn. Have it what you will. It opened up a whole box of worms. These worms have been eating away at me, waiting, growing, wanting to venture forth from my own little box. Before they do that, I will endeavour to explain the purpose of sharing my thoughts.

This is my journey, breaking out of the confines of my box; the one all of you have helped me create which includes my parents, siblings, teachers of all disciplines and our societal environment. In part, I also believe that it is like your box you have helped create for your own safety on your journey.

Further to that, I hope to explain what opening the box really means, how it can affect your whole growth process and to find out who you really are. Sharing this information does not make me an authority on the subjects discussed but only indicates where I am at this time. This is my truth at this time – tomorrow it may change. That is a wonderful thing about this life; it is continually evolving, the vistas forever widening and transforming, embracing different realities - different truths and all because of a decision to come out of that box.

Deliberate untruths occur when I have disguised the situation or the persons name to respect their privacy. Accidental untruths may also occur when my memory becomes a little hazy but then I have to try to rely on other sources of information to help clear the haze.

This book is my experience. My understanding. My truth. It does not make me an authority on the subjects discussed, but the information is based on my research, observations, conclusions and intuitive insights. It may be a starting point for you on your own pathway or it may be a signpost to give you direction. It is not *the way* but a way. Be aware on your journey that when you hear 'this way is the truth' then go another way, for then you will be released from your limitations and the limitations and dictates of others. You will be able to open and even jump out of your box.

Throughout this book, I have set aside pages of inspirations, which for me have been a creative experience, encapsulating many thoughts, emotions and situations. They are reflections of where we are (I am), where we (I) have been and the potential that is there for each of us on our Journey home. There are also passages of higher insights, (in italics) looking at situations from a different and wider perspective from the times when I have made the effort to listen to the still small voice within. The source at this stage is of no consequence, it is the content, which is of greater importance.

* * *

This is the story of my struggle to understand myself, my purpose for being here on this earth, where I am going when my number is up. Some of those answers become apparent as the story unfolds and some questions will remain unanswered until a time when I can no longer ask the question.

From a teenager I have had a feeling that I would one day write a book. During those innocent and impressionable years, I could draw on no experiences to speak of except a few of the emotions of childhood memories. Other tender emotions I kept under wraps because in a masculine world that was what was expected. At school, I had extreme difficulty in writing an essay. So unless you are blessed with an over active imagination you have to have some experience of life, not necessarily for yourself but through the eyes of another.

This is the story of the healing of an individual, which is still ongoing, who like you has experienced many trials and difficulties. It is the story of how I became a healer and of the subsequent knowledge given to me, which is to be shared, as and when and where required. The story of the healing is not in any way to be synonymous with any religious experience. It is the natural outworking of the universal law of love. It is a bit like the struggle of a seedling exerting its will on the denseness of matter, battling with the experience of the elements eventually unfolding into a beautiful flower – one small piece of the natural workings of an infinite creation.

When people think of healers, there is a tendency to think of them as something special, saintly or holy. Nothing is further from the truth. All it means is that that person has reached a certain stage on their path of spiritual progress (and is ready to come out of their box) and we are all on that same pathway. Therefore, we all have the potential to heal. It is unfortunate that over the centuries since Christ, perhaps beyond that, religious organisations have monopolised this very natural commodity for their elite in maintaining control over the populace. Leaving religion apart, the act of healing is an act of love. It is spirituality at work.

In the ensuing pages I hope to explain in simple terms how it is possible for you too to heal; yourself, your family, your community and the wonderful planet on which you have come to experience your reality and the ways you can assist in opening your box.

I do not expect that all my views and ideas will be acceptable so I say accept the things you can and reject the things you cannot, or at least put them on a shelf for the time being.

Opening The Box

Metaphorically speaking you have all been living in your own little wooden boxes and the majority still do, feeling totally secure from the conditions imposed on that box. These conditions have been imposed by society to keep each one contained within that box, so that one is aware of its parameters, each one becoming a limited expression of its true self and many are happy with that. Occasionally rebellion occurs and someone breaks out of their box creating havoc and then society creates more laws and standards to keep your boxes more secure. So the process perpetuates.

The universe has other ideas. It needs you to express yourself and show your potential as a divine being so it has sent you a host of angels to assist you in your endeavours. These angels are continually calling you and knocking on your box to weaken its structure. Its integrity is affected and the cracks in your box allow the light from outside to come into the darkness of your confinement and light up your life. You want more because it feels so good, so you lift your lid and your own light expands into all that there is out there. Many have already opened their boxes and found that freedom to express their essence, doing what their soul desires and are there to support others that are breaking free of their limitations.

Society will change, its leaders will change to bring humanity into a new understanding about itself and break down the boxes of limitation that have been built around you. No one is to blame for all that has happened or existed, it is all part of a plan — an experiment if you will, given the tools of choice and freewill.

CHAPTER I

New Beginnings

Be still and know,
to harmonise with nature will bring you close to Me,
to be part of all creation will bring you humility;
appreciate the loving that you give to mother earth,
in time she will return to you the mirror of your worth.

With a great deal of trepidation and butterflies wakening from their transformation in my stomach I slowly walked the path to a perfectly ordinary council house in the West Midlands, a walk that was to change my life. My heart had a minor tachycardia as I pushed the doorbell. A sixty-year-old sprightly woman answered, bringing with her an all-knowing smile, which partially set me at ease. She sensed my apprehension of being a first timer. She also sensed my life was in a mess.

We made our way to the little kitchen at the back of the house and seated ourselves at opposite sides of the kitchen table and she took my hands. "You are a healer", were her first words of the sitting. That was all I heard for a few moments as that phrase echoed backwards and forwards in my mind, and then as I digested them to the field of butterflies in my stomach, the rains came. I wept. And wept.

After all the turmoil in my life of recent years, of searching, trying to find some justification for my life, my prayers had been answered at last. I did not know it at the time but that eventful day in April 1981 was to change my whole way of life - and the rest of it. Once you resolve to tread your spiritual pathway there is no turning back. It is not because you have been brainwashed or under any delusions of grandeur. You are fulfilling the contract you made before you came here, outworking your destiny. It later transpired that Ruth, a medium, clairvoyant, psychic, sensitive, was to become a tremendous source of help to both my wife and myself as we journeyed along our pathway.

"I have no need to go over the past with you. You do not need proof, but you have been searching. Your emotional life is in a mess and you are terribly confused. You will give counsel to many people

9

and heal many more. There will come a time when you will not have a moment to yourself. You will give public demonstrations and will be talking from the rostrum or stage". She took my hand, began reading the hieroglyphics and confirmed all that she had already said, together with more personal details that now pale into insignificance.

I could not believe that this was going to happen to me. How could I stand up in front of a crowd of people and talk? About what? I had not at that time got the confidence to talk to half a dozen people unless it was in the work situation. My head whirled and became saturated with a multitude of questions.

"Furthermore" Ruth continued, "you have to learn patience, tolerance, and above all humility. You still have far to go, the path will be hard and cruel at times but because of what you are and what you have gone through you will succeed in whatever you set your mind to do. You were born to heal and are a natural healer".

How little I knew then, of the problems that lay ahead, of the tests that I was to endure. Patience, tolerance and discretion were (and still are) hard taskmasters.

The events leading up to this awakening were bizarre to say the least, but my wife Marion was instrumental indirectly in assisting me on my journey. Through business she was just another receptionist's voice at the end of a telephone and as often happens, you pass a few courteous words before she makes your connection.

One dreary day, six months previous I thought the world was falling apart. It was, for Marion. Over the next few days after being soaked by a deluge of tears over the airwaves, I pieced together the story of a marriage breakdown. Many of you are aware of the scenario; suffering in silence, pretending it will go away and frightened of the stigma of divorce. That is until she cracked. The worm had turned and a great deal of help came her way from diverse directions.

A friend recommended that she see a clairvoyant /medium that would help her pick up the pieces, but at that time Marion did not believe in them and that like so many others, she was frightened of the idea. Then some six weeks later, she heard a voice within cry out "See Ruth". That was enough to convince her and she arranged a meeting.

Ruth proceeded to give Marion details of all that had happened in the marital home and details of another man that has come into her life to help her. He had greying hair at the temples, was older than Marion and had two jobs, one of them connected to power or electricity. She would eventually marry again. This was of course the last thing she wanted to hear at this time. She did have some doubts because she later asked me how old I was and whether I was going grey. I was in fact (and still am) seven years younger than Marion and only had few grey ones, sparsely populated. We both breathed a sigh of relief because I did not want a lifetime of commitment either. We just became good friends and sat back lulling ourselves into a false sense of everything being all right. Remember we had not met to this time and it took me a further three months before I made an excuse to visit her.

We took Ruth to task later about 'the man she saw' being older than Marion. In spiritual terms, Ruth said I was older than Marion and the reference to power or electricity was another way of expressing the healing energy.

Prior to my visit to Ruth I sent Marion a poem I had penned previously, which even then expressed how I was feeling about my life and that somehow I needed to expand and find my potential. I had to test the water and by asking Marion to show Ruth the poem, she should be able to access information with regard to my life's purpose. Having a lot on her mind Marion forgot, but the man was there again in her reading and according to Ruth Marion was aware of him.

Ruth continued, "He is seeking a purpose in life -"

"Oh!" interrupted Marion, "I have been talking to a man on the phone. I have a poem of his he wanted you to read".

Ruth interrupted "- that doesn't matter tell him I want to see him".

About the same period as all this was going on, I engaged in conversation with a colleague at work who was involved in psychical research and for fun was a lay reader of the tarot cards. I twisted his arm for a spread. He made a few comments and said he would pass it on to an expert for analysis. It took weeks before I received the following message:

'The questioner is a sensitive, artistic and moody person. There are signs of a developed skill and an academic status. The questioner is a loner. The person is in need of spiritual fulfillment and is about to set upon a quest to quench a thirst for these needs.

GIVING

If I cannot use my talents
That were bestowed on me from birth,
If I cannot use these gifts in fulfilment
Then I have not proved my worth.

If I cannot develop all my feelings
And share them with others without greed,
If I can develop theirs in giving
Then I too know I have a need.

If I can bring a passing tear
Through a little thing said or done,
If I can share an understanding
Then I know of another battle won.

If I can dance the tune of nature
And share the life within us all,
If I can share the joy of loving
Then I have the greatest prize of all.

If I can be my Master's servant
And be part of His Divine Plan,
Then I know that place of Heaven
There will be room for a humble man.

A person will assist in this goal of fulfillment, which will be achieved without financial gain or profit, but with much happiness. The path will be hurtful but so rewarding'.

I remember feeling apprehensive at the time but I did have that deep desire to find and fulfill my destiny. Surprisingly the interpretation gave me a real sense of hope. It showed me facets of my character that were true and of the traumas that lay ahead. The developed skill I did not understand at the time but later assumed it referred to the healing.

Four months later brought me to Ruth's doorstep once again. I was having problems with the healing and various individuals but I suppose I wanted some more of her 'encouragement'.

"Relaxation is important and not to exist as a personality. You must have periods of calm", was the essence of my enquiry.

I could not get it where I was living or at work so when I was able took myself to the great outdoors, to commune with nature. Communing, being and feeling part of our natural world gave me the necessary boost to soldier on and somehow brought me closer to the essence of what God is all about. I would encourage anyone who feels dispirited, dejected, to make a conscious effort to be alone and walk alone, appreciating the natural beauty that surrounds you and if it makes you feel so much better, talk to the birds and flowers (mentally in case anyone is watching), become at one with them.

"You must clear your mind of earthly problems. You have a strong destiny, there is much more to come. You will be a leader in a spiritual way. You must hold back your impatience".

Impatience. This was the bane of my life. Everything had to be completed yesterday. In work or play, I applied myself and expected everyone else to do the same. It took a lot of heartache and suffering to relinquish the hold this beast had on me but eventually with the help of self-healing techniques, meditation (and Marion's calming influence) over the years, I have become calmer and more patient. Yet I still have my mad moments especially when I feel inspired or on the odd occasion when I feel, someone is not moving as fast as they might be, although I know each has to move at their own pace.

"You will have a greater understanding of fellow man and see them as they really are, but it will all take time. You will leave your employment eventually to heal full time, but this is well into the future".

My box had opened just a little. Just enough for me to assimilate the next stage of my journey for there was much I had to learn.

The desire to heal also became quite an obsession. For so long I was biting at the bit to do something with my life and heal the world. Not for an ego trip but for the fact I had something I could share to help relieve the suffering and illnesses that plague humanity. There were many happenings yet to take place before I could really appreciate the potential of the words that were shared with me. There were facets of my character that needed to be remoulded and a great deal of self-healing and healing within my own family.

CHAPTER 2

The Wilderness Years

Be still and know,
that on your life's journey there are many things to learn,
at each and every crossroad you have to take a turn;
remember as you walk this path of happiness, sorrow and fear,
you will always see an ending because I am always near.

Before we continue with the healing story I feel it is important to share some of my roots, background and some of the effects, situations and people have had on my existence. Let us first dispel any thoughts that people may have, with respect to healers being holy or saintly to fulfil their role as healers. The pillars of the religious establishments have fostered this attitude of mind unfortunately, in their efforts to maintain control and autonomy of healing. As I hope to demonstrate, the capacity to heal is within all of us. If you have the capacity to love, to have compassion for a fellow being you have the essential qualities required of a healer.

It all began for me on 30th January 1944, during an air raid on the east end of London. I came out coughing and continued that way during my early years, which included long friendships with kaolin poultices, X-ray machines and candles under my nose. I had eyes in the seat of my trousers so I had to kid myself I could see people coming up behind me. On occasions, there was gang warfare in the streets. Why they developed I will never know, but after a while my elder brother and I did not have many opponents. It did not end up there; we invariably ended up starting our own wars between ourselves, which was terminated with lashings of my father's belt. Dad was strict with discipline and backed it up with his leather tongue. I have no regrets in being chastised in such a way, I am sure it did me a power of good. It would after all be a waste of breath trying to reason with a little rebel. Whilst now I would not agree with such forms of punishment, that reason should always prevail, discipline is always necessary for a child's growth, that child needs to know about boundaries in order to learn to form moral judgments.

It was difficult for mum and dad in those early postwar years, bringing up four children (later five) but we were kept clean and always had food in our stomachs. They tried their best with the resources they had at their disposal. My father and I have not always agreed about many things mainly about issues of control but from my perspective now, I can say I have no regrets about the events that turned my life around, only the hurt I had caused. Spiritually we all agreed on our contracts before we came here, from a personal standpoint to teach me the things I needed to know and understand, to enable me to cope with the experience the rest of humanity were to give me. I thank my parents for that.

One quality my father developed unconsciously with all of us was stubbornness. For me that quality developed into a determination that helped me shape a career and a gentle assertiveness that is so often required when dealing with the problems of others. Mum was a gentle person. What she may have lacked in education, she more than made up in compassion. She cared. Unfortunately in the family circumstances she did not realise her full potential. In hindsight, I can see why most of the developments took place the way they did in my early years, as happens with all of us. Sometimes people say and do things that may be hurtful, but to help let go of those regrets is to say we did not know any better at the time. Developing that attitude of mind allows you to put those hurts at rest.

As you would love your parents, because of their endearing ways or through obligatory blood ties, would it not be more loving to detach yourself and relate to them, as two friends, who have joyfully provided the opportunity for you to experience this dimension, bringing you to this moment? You owe them nothing but your thanks. Similarly, your child owes you nothing. If you provided the early guidance that that child needed, together with the freedom of expression, encouraging that power within the child to express itself as a creative spark of the divine, then you too have fulfilled your purpose.

The next phase began when we moved to Basildon, a new town in Essex taking overspill from London's east end. It was all countryside then, I learnt the hard way what stinging nettles were and the beneficial effect of dock leaves, which formulated my early introduction to herbalism! I also found that cows, ducks and pigs were live animals and that not all cowpats were solid. Likewise, I'd walk the crust of a pond that had dried up and found out that Jesus was a very special person. On one occasion a friend and I were caught, lifting a few eggs from a farm chicken shed, well those chicks had a premature birth because those eggs grew wings. I received my due punishment, a double dose, for attempting to steal and for making extra washing! Pushing the barriers of chance enabled me to develop a fair turn of speed and in later years represent the school at athletics and other sports. Therefore some good came from my early endeavours.

I developed into more of a loner in my early teens, certainly by choice but indirectly through one of the major turning points in my life. It was during those days that every aspiring pupil sat the eleven-plus for a grammar school education and I was considered to be near the front of the queue. I failed. I failed the re-sit. I failed the thirteen-plus after being at the top of the class at secondary school. It was down to butterflies! These failures unleashed a fury within, a stark determination to prove the system wrong, that someone from the working class can make the grade. I was to carry this chip on my shoulder for the next fifteen years. I worked and studied hard, as this rebel had a cause and at the age of twenty-six, qualified as a Member of the Institution of Municipal Engineers followed by Membership of the Institution of Civil Engineers and the status of chartered engineer.

There are no regrets now, about the way life had been so unjust although it felt like it at the time. It was as though I was being taught in another school and that somehow I had to learn the qualities of application and determination to succeed. Unfortunately, these qualities gave birth to arrogance and the need to demonstrate that I was right. This landed me on another and much steeper learning curve.

In my early twenties, I left my parental home amidst a storm of differing opinions, mainly between my father and myself. It stayed that way for nearly fifteen years. For me they were painful years as I am sure they were for my parents and siblings, lonely years, but my stubborn pride and arrogance prevented me from giving way. There were more lessons I still had to learn like charity and humility, how to respect persons and property, be less materialistic and how to be a little more loving to fellow man.

NOBODY'S FOOL

These calloused hands so tired and torn
Are tools of battles in a world of scorn,
Scarring the rock of many a hill
In rewarding one to have his fill.

They have remodelled men from the clay
Moulding their future for a better way,
Delicately they have held the sweet breath of life
And carved a love with whittling knife.

They have given their all with open heart
Joining with others never to part.
As in holding they are part of giving
And share with them the joy of living.

They have penned the way of fruitful psalms
And one day when in another's palms,
The message will come from the holy hall
That these hands of mine were nobody's fool.

During my willful teenage years I turned away from God, how unjust he was, how unchristian people were, how there was so much strife in the world. In fact, these atheistic years helped wipe my slate clean with respect to the teachings of religious orthodoxy and helped open up my mind to what life is really all about. I found my own way back to God eventually, through my years in the wilderness, experiencing a closeness to the natural order of things, and conveying my thoughts into the medium of poetry. I did not particularly enjoy poetry at school, I could not understand most of it, but the pieces I was inspired to write amazed me. In retrospect now, I realise that I was receiving spiritual inspirations and some of the poems were even prophetic in their content.

On occasions, I wrote 'pieces' for others, perhaps to help them in their moments of despair. Others found me out, mainly women, who wanted to discuss some emotional crisis or love issue. I did not always feel qualified to help since my own love life, apart from a few escapades, had been negligible but I was a people watcher and somehow experienced life through other dilemmas. I was a bit of a romantic as well.

I wrote to myself on many occasions to express how I really felt. I despaired many times, became introverted socially but I realize now I had to hit rock bottom for me to really appreciate life. The times clients have crossed my path not enjoying the mess they have made of their lives, all following the same pattern and the times I have said, " Keep holding the vision that it will not get any worse and one day you will really appreciate the happiness that comes your way". I feel that by experiencing the dark end of the spectrum of life can you really appreciate the other. The deeper the suffering the greater the happiness, one is relative to the other. That is a truth.

During those wilderness years, I wrote: 'Where lies my destiny of a spirit fulfilled? I do need to know of the path that I must follow in the knowledge that my spiritual self may develop and blossom before the parting of the ways.

'I have searched, through determination of effort to be a qualified success, through the adolescent years of agnosticism, the painful years of materialism and found myself wanting. I suppose deep down the only way I can satisfy my hunger pains is to find and accept God,

THIS IS

A gentle nod, an open palm
This is love that is always calm,
The sparkling eye, the tender touch
This is love but none too much.
A quiet voice, an open heart
This is love that can never part,
The cheery smile, the tender kiss
This is love that should not miss.
This is the stuff of which dreams are made,
This is love that will never fade,
It remains here forever all our days
This is love now and always.
This love is like a flower in curls
Revealing a nature as each petal unfurls,
Something rarely seen and never heard
Yet equally free on the wing of a bird,
This is love that tastes so sweet,
This is love no more to meet.

whoever and whatever He/She/It is. I need guidance along my spiritual pathway. I know and feel that I have untapped potential I need to share. I also have the gift of love, the same as everyone; perhaps I should work at that. How? Humility. I feel humble when I marvel at the workmanship of the world of nature but I look at humanity and my heart cries out with pain.

'Lately I have been even more aware of Him, perhaps because of my own personal distress. That sounds selfish but it has taken all these years for me to realise the truth of His patience, tolerance, understanding and wisdom. If I can for humanity's sake, be just one small link in His infinite chain of procreation.

'As each year passes by I have a greater need to love and to be part of God, to express that essence. That must be my destiny. In a strange way, I feel I have an obligation to society, to humanity, to God.

'I have wasted so much time and there is so much work to be done. I feel if I were to be of service in some way, it would help me understand, be more tolerant, to have continual awareness, to be at peace'.

In another of my more sombre moments when I was actually feeling quite ill, I was inspired to write 'There Came a Tapping'.

This I hope conveys the state of desperation I had reached in my evolution without going into the details as to the reasons, suffice it is to say I feel I attracted everything that came my way. The net result is that you learn from your mistakes; not whether you have won or lost or whether you were right or wrong. My schooling had not finished, I just found myself in a different classroom.

THERE CAME A TAPPING

There came a tapping on my door
So quiet at first it seemed,
I opened wide to see far more
To make sure I hadn't dreamed.

Some visions passed me by just then
Of beauty and such wealth,
I closed the door and wondered when
I could restore my health.

There came a banging on my door
I held it just ajar,
It was much louder than before
And outside I saw a star.

It shone so bright it took my sight
My body it gave me pain,
I turned my back and then took flight
So I shut my door again.

There came a thundering on my door
My soul cried out with fear,
My body lay wretched on the floor
My mind was far from clear.

The door burst open, night descended
No beauty could beheld,
My body then could not be mended
Because my heart had gelled.

My soul inside bore up to leave
Tearing my life apart,
My lifeless body began to heave
And pumped blood into my heart.

Then I remembered the sweetest song
Said in times of need,
To pray to God to right the wrong
And sow more fertile seed

So I prayed for just a little while
And wept for far much more,
Then I talked and raised a little smile
And all was quiet at my door.

I thank you God for showing how
That I can be a part,
For I have learned my lesson now
Secure within my heart.

CHAPTER 3

On The Road

Be still and know,
when you are all alone then call on Me by name.
talk with Me - the feeling is just the same:
share with Me your burdens so that I may lend a hand,
to give you time for gathering the strength to make a stand.

There were many problems during those early years of healing, many of them through my own making. I was impatient for action and too willing an advocate for my new cause. The motives behind those qualities may have been creditable but I made many mistakes through my excess of enthusiasm. I appreciate now how much remoulding was necessary.

A few books about other healers passed through my hands but none of them really told me how I should go about it. Such questions as to where to put your hands and for how long plagued my mind. My first client Len, a colleague at work had an old back injury and while I was working on him, I asked him if he felt anything. His response was negative. I could not feel anything either and after a few sessions I began to think someone was being conned. Unknowingly, my desire to heal, to cure, got in the way. I so much wanted a positive result. I knew that laid back Len had no barriers to what I was trying to achieve, in fact, he was instrumental a few years previously to introduce me to the concept of healing. My knowledge up to that moment was limited to the big man two thousand years ago.

At that time, I developed a frozen shoulder with excruciating pain. Driving became unbearable and medication had little effect. Len suggested I might try a healer. He knew of one several years back and would make enquiries. It took a few weeks and finally traced the woman who played a small but very important part of my life. Five sessions later my shoulder had melted! I remembered on my last session as it was feeling easier I commented, 'I would love to be able to do this'.

It was some while later that there was a response to my request as though it was part of some plan beyond my comprehension.

My next two guinea pigs were also colleagues from work. Jeff had a 'bad' shoulder and after a few minutes felt ninety percent better. A few more minutes the next day cleared the condition. Ron had been off work for six weeks with shingles and had popped in for some information still feeling quite distressed. After a few words, he was open to anything. That was a Thursday or Friday. The following Monday he was back at work with no more symptoms and the sores cleared quickly leaving no scar tissue.

At last, I was on the road, but it did get a bit bumpy at times.

It is amazing how word spreads even when you try to be careful. It always invariably provides someone with ammunition, to shoot back at you. Offices are hotbeds for gossip though I did not find that out until later. Word got around and you may hear a facetious remark as you passed by someone, or you received word from a supporter that someone was up to no good. In retrospect I only blame myself, perhaps I should have been a little more discreet. I read somewhere that when you have something to say that someone may take exception to, build your fences first. Have the courage of your convictions, ignore the ignorance and no one can hurt you. I was hurt at times but turned the other cheek and soldiered on.

I received a challenge a few years later. Towards the end of one day, I went to the assistance of a colleague in another department who had severe arthritis. I volunteered to assist (I had given him healing previously) and we found a quiet room away from the maddening crowd. I thought I was being discreet, but the next day I received a reprimanded for my action. The office grapevine worked true to form, but this time to my advantage. There was to be an enquiry and a union representative came forward to represent me. Now I did not believe in trade unions and had refused to join one, but this kind soul came forward to speak on my behalf (because he had been one of my patients!) and after an enquiry (and a few intimidating comments) I was given a verbal warning.

I did not think I deserved that, considering I was going to someone's aid although it may not have been exactly urgent and in works time. I reminded the enquiry of the parable of the good Samaritan, which went down like a brick. I also knew if that issue was going to cost me my job the press would have had a field day.

THE HIGHWAY

That as you travel your own highway
Falling by the wayside in despair,
Call on me for I will carry you
For a time you know not where.

I will take you to my kingdom
And heal you of your ill,
Mend you of your broken heart
And build upon your will.

You will come to recognise
With the passing of your time,
That despair is but an obstacle
On the special hill you climb.

You will walk again your highway
With experience you have gained,
Of despair and of the tears
And the days when it had rained.

You will come upon a stranger
Lying hurt upon the road,
Lift him up with all my love
And carry his full load.

You can comfort him and heal him
And make him good as new,
Sharing the love that I AM
That I have given you.

Perhaps it was a bit of one-upmanship on my part but as a sequel to these events, I elected to become one of the department's first aid officers. The chief first aid officer agreed that when necessary after using orthodox techniques, I might use any other techniques to bring relief to the condition as I might think appropriate! A first aid room was available, to which I made frequent use.

Fortunately, now with the increased interest in complementary therapies and healing, individuals are less likely to ridicule those working on the fringe.

Sometimes I found people's attitude to faith provided a barrier for any healing to occur, particularly if they had keen religious convictions. Faith is not necessary for a healing to occur although it may certainly assist in the process. Both animals and children have been treated the world over, with success, so how can it be said that faith is necessary? I have also treated sceptics with successful outcomes, only because their partners had implored them to give healing a try.

One particular woman who had no faith or belief in healing had injured her lower back and the consequent pain was unbearable. She was unable to sit or bend and suffered many sleepless nights. After five minutes of healing and with my heart in my mouth, I suggested that she gently touch her toes. She stared at me unbelievingly and hesitatingly did as I asked. Her mouth dropped open and her face awash with tears of relief. Her husband and I shared in her joy!

At the other extreme another patient who I saw a few years later, had the utmost faith in what I was doing. She appeared to be relaxed but the healing had no effect after a fifteen-minute session. This confused me but I accepted the outcome. It was only after we were conversing she mentioned she was praying all the time during the session. I nearly went spare. Relaxing means just that. A personal prayer before commencement may be helpful, but in my experience a parrot repetition coming from the mind and not the heart does not really produce the desired results.

It is so advisable for both healer and patient to relax to allow the forces of healing to have maximum effect. If the healer can spend time talking to the patient before commencing, helping them unwind can assist the flow of energy.

A dramatic consequence of this occurred when visiting a patient who had continual jaw ache, which was not surprising because I could not get a word in edgeways. He also had occasional headaches. After spending half an hour listening I suggested that we start healing at which he replied that his pains had disappeared!

Similar reactions have occurred whilst giving public demonstrations and talks to groups about healing. Members of the audience have remarked on a different occasions that they came in with a pain or discomfort and by the end of the talk it had disappeared. Sometimes it is not necessary to touch, but by the healer just being there the healing vibrations are all that is necessary to effect a relief. It also means that that person is at that moment in time ready to receive healing.

Another problem that gave me grief was where to put my hands and for how long. I had read of other healers who had experienced pain exactly where the patient was suffering and of others who intuitively felt where to place their hands. Since I could feel neither of these 'clues', and could feel no heat or sensations in my hands initially I felt I was not doing the job properly. It was not until later that I could 'scan' the body with one of my hands and pick up hot spots, which indicated to me they were the areas requiring attention. These areas did not necessarily coincide with the site of the pain but relief could still be effective. I learned later that these hotspots might also indicate a blockage in the energy system.

My early years on the road were tiring. I chose to visit clients after work and sometimes, since I lived some distance away, arrived home late, exhausted. It was not the healing that was tiring it was all the travelling around after a day at work. That gave rise to another of my problems.

Prior to, and at the time of my mid life crisis I had been living with friends who had endured my mood swings for some years, as I had theirs. I shared with them the fact that I had seen a clairvoyant and the enlightening news I received. The ridicule I received was beyond expectation. I could not believe that close friends who could show such compassion at times could be so discouraging. After a few months and many soul-searching deliberations, I collected my few worldly possessions and was away.

Later I was to understand why others with whom you have

travelled no longer have an affinity with you.

You may have reached a point where their energies cannot contribute to your own growth. If their energies are such that you are disturbed by their presence in that emotions of anger, resentment and hate are raised then yes, there is still much you can learn, to deal with your own emotions. If you feel compassionate because of their circumstances, you may assist in their growth if that is their wish. There is usually a reason why other people are attracted to you or you to them. There may be other circumstances of contact brought about by others in an indirect way. These beings may refuse to move out of their space. That is their choice. Recognise that this is their way and you should respect that they have chosen the road they travel. You may send them light and love to assist them on their journey but it is not for you to involve yourself in their scenario. This will only bring conflict. It is true that if you are truly within your own space that conflict will not affect your being, but where conflict is generated it is best isolated and left to burn itself out when no fuel is added to the fire.

So do not feel the pangs of guilt as you turn away from another being in these circumstances. Allow your compassion and love to flow from your being as you separate. They may not understand that point on their journey but that energy will always be with them and will mark its target and fuse with the spark of divinity that lies within that being at the appropriate time. Their time is not your time. Allow it to be so.

The important lesson here was that no person has the right to dictate to another, as to what that person should and should not do. It is a violation of freedom of choice. Responsibilities come in there somewhere but when a person is on their own pathway to spiritual fulfillment, no one has the right to hold them back. It is amazing how often this does occur and invariably it is the female half of a relationship that wants to move forward, and the male tries to hold their partner back, maybe because of their own insecurity and sense of fear or loss.

THANK YOU

Thank you God for those sunny days
When we did all but care,
And for those moments of reflection
The ones we couldn't share.

Thank you dear God for being fair
In being just to me,
Thank you also for opening my eyes
In the face of adversity.

Thank you dear God for this life
And all the lessons learnt,
Of trials and prejudices
that scorn and anger burnt.

Most of all dear God I have you to thank
In my darkest hour of need,
That in that fleeting moment
I know that you will lead.

Because I know that all the suffering
That I bring upon my soul,
Will being me one step nearer
Towards the greatest goal

CHAPTER 4

Interpretation

Be still, and know,
that when you pray I hear every word,
when you cry from the heart it goes not unheard;
I will answer your call when the time is right,
when your candle is ready to yield more light.

In 1984, I received an invitation to give my first talk and demonstration to a women's guild. Without any preparation, I naively I thought I would receive direct guidance from spirit. After a few minutes introduction, I began to dry up with embarrassment so I asked a volunteer to be able to demonstrate (hopefully) the effect of healing. While I was working, some bright spark wanted to ask some questions to which I readily agreed. Other questions followed and this formed a format for subsequent talks, so perhaps I did receive guidance indirectly.

For some while, Marion sat at the back of the groups taking notes of the questions and my performance. This improved delivery and eventually we had a regular format for future various evening talks and demonstrations.

Now I mentioned earlier about my non-capacity to talk to groups partially because of an inherent shyness. My desire to share healing assisted in overcoming this obstacle. I have found and it applies to everybody, that when you speak from the heart it flows. The love you have for the love you share is the juice that makes it taste so sweet.

In 1984 after a platonic friendship developing into an emotional tug of war, Marion and I tied the knot on the hottest day of the year. Previously, we were out driving one day, discussing our proposals when unexpectedly, I said that she would be wearing pink on the day and that her accessories would be two-tone. She said she was not too keen on pink and as for two-tone accessories…

Within a few days, she received a pink outfit from her sister in South Africa. She hunted everywhere for shoes and handbag and eventually she found a two-tone beige match in Scotland!

Marion also received a few inspirations prior to the great event. She had a dream one night the wedding ring would not come off her finger, so she begged me so that she could wear it for a night. I relented and sure enough the next day we nearly had to bring in a surgeon or the fire brigade! We changed it for a larger size. One day she had a vision of her fainting at the wedding ceremony whilst making her vows. At the appropriate moment during the actual ceremony, she could not respond and her brother and I were actually supporting each arm. I naturally put it down to nervous tension or else I was too much for her. Therefore, what happened, another premonition fulfilled!

There were a number of times we received help from spirit which was to form a long and intermittent association. They are always there and will try to assist if you ask them, as long as the motive is right and if it is for our highest good. There were times when one of us might suggest something that would be useful and then we would forget about it. Once Marion suggested we should put some sweet peas in the garden and I had squashed the idea saying it was too late for planting out. A few days later as the postman was making his delivery he asked if we would like some sweet pea plants! This philosophy taught me to develop patience and if anything would help us, it would come our way. The bigger things took a little longer, especially when we were looking for the appropriate property in mid Wales for a healing centre, but that is another story (see Chapter 7).

Just prior to and into the early years of our marriage Marion and I visited a number of clairvoyants / tarot readers / mediums, mainly seeking further clarification on the work that lay ahead and to satisfy our underlying hunger to know more. A lot of the information was insignificant and shaded by what Ruth had already revealed. We taped most of the sittings and I cannot emphasise too strongly the importance of recordings rather than rely on memory. Due to personal desires and needs, the mind does not always hear what it wants to or only selects information that it needs (the sort of thing men sometimes do) and discards the rest. We found by experiment, that by independently writing down after the meeting what we thought we heard and comparing it with the tape recording, we had three differing interpretations. If a reader is reluctant about recording the session because of possibilities of litigation then they are insecure in the work that they do and should perhaps not be practicing.

One of the most important points to consider quite clearly is that of interpretation. Very often, a lot of information picked up by clairvoyants is in the form of symbols and pictures. The receiver interprets these for the client. You may read your notes or listen to the tape recording a few weeks later and arrive at another interpretation. Further on in time when a particular event takes place, it may occur to you that that was the actual meaning of the message. Therefore, it is important to seek clarification at the time of the sitting and keep your mind open to other possibilities. Also, do not tie yourself down to timescales. In spiritual terms, time does not exist. This is very difficult to conceive with our limited intellect. In the spiritual dimension especially at the higher levels, it is as though the past and future exist in the present, so when we ask 'when is it going to happen', you will appreciate that it will be difficult to be exact since there is no yardstick to measure by.

The information also given at a certain time relates only to the circumstances at that time. Situations can change depending on our free will and choice, whether we go right or left can alter the timing of an anticipated event. We therefore can make decisions that can cause delays to our individual destinies. Some events relating to our destinies are part of a prearranged plan that would be beneficial for our soul growth, but we may choose not to face a situation, causing a delay. That is exactly what it is, a delay. If that event is intended for your soul growth, it will still happen in some form, at some time in the future.

A great deal of information given by mediums appears to be irrelevant or trite certainly among spectators or congregations in spiritualist's churches. This irrelevant information is deliberate in its intent, in that it only intended for the recipient and can bring about a greater depth of understanding. Sometimes information transmitted in these circumstances is of a very personal nature, which may bring home an important truth to the receiver.

During this period of gathering and disseminating information, it seemed incredible that there seemed a whole army of people from other dimensions willing to give of themselves in some way to assist us on our journey. Through their earthly development, they had acquired a quality of character, which they could use to assist us energetically. If we needed patience or perhaps a calming influence, a nun may come forward or even a member of your own family who possessed that quality of spirit.

Invariably, during my healing apprenticeship, (I use that term loosely since we never stop learning) I was inundated with help from doctors, nurses, surgeons, and herbalists. All these beings were there to assist me or work through me whilst I was healing. From my researches on the subject, most spiritual healers have similar assistants, who wish to continue with their work in spirit in order to assist in healing humanity. I have not always been aware of who in spirit was working with me at a particular time, but sometimes there have been spates of a particular type of illness such as arthritis or spinal injuries, which would tend to indicate a specialist in that field has come to assist in the healing process.

CHAPTER 5

Circles

Be still and know,
that when on earth while you are living
in sharing My love in all that you do,
by giving and caring for every soul
will bring many gifts to you.
Faith, hope and truth are a few
of the building blocks you earn,
to take you forward with wisdom and love
you took the trouble to learn.

Following Ruth's suggestion for more inner calm and after meeting up with a local healer, whom Ruth had also put on the road, my answer seemed to be to follow the path of meditation. What it was I did not really know, only that it was something to do with being still and quiet, which would help me develop. After making discreet enquiries, I located a group in Birmingham, run by a lovely friendly couple that welcomed me into their thriving group of eight / ten souls all at various stages of development.

I was briefly told what to do at that first meeting, "Just give off whatever comes into your mind, and if you feel it is for a particular person get up and go over to them." Well I did not have a clue. I sat quietly for a few meetings, watched and listened as the messages pass from one to another. Well, I felt a bit out of it, until I started to get the shakes. Whether it was a nervous reaction on my part, or whether my guide had a bit of a dilemma with my energy field, I could not say. My fellow students just told me to "Give it off". If I had, they would have heard a lot more that evening that would not have sounded very spiritual.

It came to a head some three months later when our glorious leader said that a few of the group were not doing enough to enhance their development. I assumed he was referring to me, so at the end of the evening I said my gratuitous farewells.

So what came out of this experience for me? It was a start at least.

In hindsight, I would have taken me aside and given me a separate introduction into meditation, explaining more about it and its benefits. In fact, that is what I do now if a fledgling needs to grow a few feathers. It is so important for a beginner to understand the principles of flight before he leaves the nest. There was another factor at the time that brought about some rebelliousness. I was determined not going to be controlled by anyone or anything. In my naivety, this attitude may well have put up some sort of barrier to my development. If explanations were given at the time then my development may have made more rapid progress. But as I have previously echoed, my pathway has been littered with boulders and obstacles, some of them my own creations but in essence if it is worth the effort then you will not forget the experience.

I took to meditating alone after that experience or sometimes with Marion when the situation permitted. A few years down the road after we were married, we meditated regularly as soon as we awoke for probably twenty-minute sessions.

With a few years behind me on the circuit, delivering a few talks and demonstrations I felt moved to be a little more ambitious and start our own meditation group.

In April 1985, I elected to facilitate a healing demonstration at a studio theatre in Stafford. It went well with over forty attending; part of my reasoning in spite of the minor anti-demonstration outside was to gauge the general interest in healing and to ascertain if anyone was interested in joining a meditation group. It turned out that thirteen were interested which whittled down to about five after a few weeks. Of these, one couple were informed by a medium in Lancashire a year or so before, that they would be joining a meditation group and a clairvoyant in Kent told the other couple that they would be joining a group led by someone called Robinson! This had also occurred before I decided to venture along this particular pathway of running a meditation group.

Now none of us had much of an idea about how a group should operate but we decided initially to sit quietly for an hour and then share our visions, thoughts and perceptions. We followed this road for a while until Monica started going deeper into her meditations, experiencing clearer visions and feelings and talking directly to discarnate beings.

Now Monica was a lovely rotund person, very self-effacing with a down to earth humour we all enjoyed before and after our group sessions.

Suddenly one evening in a deeper state, she started to pant heavily and cried for help. We all opened our eyes except for Monica and I wondered was going on. I hesitatingly asked what the matter was. It turned out that the person who was speaking through Monica was an athlete who had collapsed and died whilst running, was frightened and was totally beside himself. He had in fact suffered a heart attack and had not realised he had died. I joined in his scenario called for an ambulance and gave him comfort as we went to hospital. Monica awoke naturally as though nothing had happened.

Each week we convened the theme continued. Someone had died, usually in traumatic circumstances. Some knew they were dead but were lost and felt a prayer would help and it usually did. Someone, usually a relative who had moved on to the spiritual realms, came to meet them. For some months we continued not knowing what we were really doing and Monica was totally out of it! Enquiries from spiritualist circles suggested that we might have as a rescue circle. This began to make sense. It became apparent that where some souls depart this life in a state of shock or trauma, or have some sort of emotional tie with the earth-life they become trapped in their emotional turmoil and are not able to move on into the lighter spiritual realms. How these beings find their way to rescue circles is still unanswered but they are somehow attracted to the spiritual light generated by the group. All that is required is for a member of the group to link up with them, taking them to meet a deceased relative and by suggestion create a situation to assist them to move on into the light.

There have been a number of occasions where the spirit has felt trapped, or in a state of limbo. Because of the state of mind, possibly through a burden of guilt at the time of passing, the trauma has left them in a state of darkness, as though they are in a total darkened room. You can suggest that they are in a room and hence a room has a door. You may also suggest that there is a keyhole in that door, through which there appears a thin beam of light. You ask them to go to that beam and open the door into the light where their friends or relatives are waiting for them. It is so essential therefore, that those who are ready to pass should be encouraged to go in peace and to let go of earthly connections.

One visitation (through Monica) came through in trauma, reported seeing a ball of fire and being engulfed in flames. He asked us to pray for him and all the others when it happened. This confused us at first since the event had yet to take place. Several days later, many people all over the world were emotionally affected by the aircraft disaster at Locherbie, Scotland. We received no concrete evidence to relate our visitation to Locherbie so we reasonably assumed that this was so, since no other similar incidents made the news headlines. We also assumed that this being was another aspect of the man that died in the holocaust and that the traumatic event was probably predestined and could not have been prevented. On coming out of her deep trance, Monica reported a distinct burnt taste in her mouth but had no recollection of the message that she conveyed.

On another occasion, we were in the presence of one of the early kings of England prior to the introduction of Christianity. Although he refused to give his name, (arrogantly stating that if I was in his court I should know) Monica was given the scenario before she went deeper into trance and from her description of the costume the period (from her own research later) appeared to be around 600 A.D. Furthermore, from my discreet questioning he appeared not to have heard of or converted to Christianity. He accepted healing for his sore foot and drifted off to sleep. Why this soul should still be stuck in his reality for such a long time we will never know, but perhaps the healing he experienced through Monica may have led him to ask a few questions from his attached reality.

Sadly, Monica passed from this life with ovarian cancer a few years after John her husband passed, who was also a stalwart of our small group. She was instrumental as a trance medium in carrying out some stirring work in helping many lost souls and we thank her sincerely for sharing that experience with us.

We plodded on with our home group, developing slowly until Linda joined us. She had joined a development group at the local spiritualist church and met up with an ego that tried to dictate to her what she should and should not do. With this discomfort behind her, the grapevine directed her to us and remained with us until we disbanded our group.

Linda predominately developed as a clairvoyant and cheerfully accepted comments on her presentation and delivery. Occasionally she too would drift off into deeper trance and we would once again assume our role as a rescue circle.

Our next lift off with our home groups occurred in 1992.

Just after we started a weekly evening healing centre at Stafford the spiritualist movement decided to convene a meeting (coincidence or what?) to ascertain the local interest in starting a church. Out of common interest, we decided to go along.

The meeting went quite well, backed up with a few demonstrations of clairvoyance and they subsequently started a church. What became of interest to me directly was that one of the mediums that I was talking to after the proceedings asked me if I had heard about the ascension tapes. I had not, so she briefly explained about the process. We left it that she would send me a few cassette tapes. This did not strike me as being particularly significant until a few minutes later, another person involved in personal development and in whom I had a great respect asked me the same question.

The bells started ringing. If there is one thing I had learnt from the beginning of my quest, if events, statements, actions came together in rapid succession then stop and listen. I listened to those tapes, channelled by an American Eric Klein and I cried buckets. It was as though I was receiving a wake-up call for the next part of my journey. I will endeavour to explain more about this process later, (see chapter 20) but I was so impressed with the concepts and ideas I facilitated a workshop with two others a few months later. Resulting from the interest, we started another home group, a monthly ascension group that lasted until just before we left Stafford. The essence of this group was that it was to be a discussion group with meditation and opportunities for individuals to channel with the high energies developed within the group. At times, we crushed up to thirty people into two adjoining rooms and had as many as six channelling in one session. It provided a great opportunity for people with like minds to come together, with some travelling distances of over thirty miles to enjoy an enlightening experience.

Holding and running these groups was a wonderful growing experience for both Marion and me. We wanted ultimately to develop a healing centre and all that we experienced was an education, learning to maintain a degree of control in your own home and sometimes gently having to remind others how to respect property.

CHAPTER 6

Centres

Be still and know,
all the gifts from me that make me part of you
can only grow and blossom if you can flower too;
it is the sharing of these gifts - the ones you cannot see,
like the giving and the loving that brings you close to me.

After a few years on the road giving talks and demonstrations to various clubs, groups and women's institutes locally, I felt the desire to expand more, going further a field to share my truth and experience. By one of those accidents or quirks of fate, someone told me about a centre in the west midlands that were involved in healing, yoga and were saying and doing all the right things. I just had to investigate.

The meetings of thirty to forty people packed into a small room, was electric with love energy. Birthday celebrations had generous helpings of songs and hugs – the most wonderful therapy of all. We kept on the perimeter of this group as its charismatic energy swept round the U.K. especially in yoga circles. We could see more of what was happening with the dynamics of the group regarding opening up and procurement. They wanted expansion and it did.

It was true. They were expressing what people wanted to hear and feel such as nutrition, health, complementary therapies, and love. It was all there. Based on yogic principles, of which I had not a clue, the centre's foundations were based on eastern philosophy. Its leader was of Indian descent, a charismatic gentle soul who exuded love. He said all the right things and certainly what people needed to hear, Marion and I included. Many of the followers and those involved in the group regarded him as their guru.

It was there I drew the line. The interpretation of guru means 'one who shines the light'. He was in that sense, but the way women seem to swoon over him (and some men) and hang on to every word as though it was the gospel left us cold. It is a complete responsibility shift by allowing someone to control your life. Many that are lost do need help, to take responsibility for their selves and I feel that it should be the responsibility of any 'guru' to show them that pathway. This is where the system, I feel fell a little short of its objectives. Unfortunately there were I felt, other shortfalls. There are with any organisations. We went on a few weekend retreats with the ever-expanding enterprise to a cottage they obtained in North Wales, because we were learning so much, the positive and the negative.

It is difficult to be non-judgemental in such circumstances but we critically observed and kept our observations intact. It was indeed a learning curve for us. We knew the things we would not do when the time came to have an open house healing centre. Unfortunately, there appeared to be from some quarters a disrespect of property and a lack of sharing in the chores. Nevertheless, we had a lot of fun.

A real fun week was a retreat with other inspired searchers on Bardsey Island off the Lleyn peninsula, North Wales. The guru and a few of his assistants came as well. Bardsey is a beautiful tranquil setting, a place of pilgrimage in ancient times. Our accommodation was very spartan, so was the toilet, a small shack and a bucket, which we were to take turns in emptying. Paper was scarce, particularly since our billet was also the meeting place for meditations, therapies and other activities. We went on nightly forays to the other houses to balance the situation. The situation worsened by the end of the week, when food was also running short and supplemented by available wild diet, which resulted in excessive use of the shack. One morning one of our cohabiters took an inordinately long time to complete her business. On evacuation of the shack, she said she had an explosive mishap and had to clean the walls without the use of running water.

Another accomplishment Marion and I shared at that time was writing a song. Now I always had a burning desire to put some of my poetry to music but with being unable to engage the tune in my brain with my mouth, I was unable to deliver the required output. Marion had no musical background but a lovely soft voice. Therefore, I penned a few words, inspired by my natural surroundings and asked Marion to go away and see what comes. She returned sooner than I expected, sufficiently inspired. We immediately took our combined effort to our resident guitarist and he produced the music. That was not all. The next day none of us could remember the tune, but after flogging it for a few hours, it came back and produced it for our finale at the end of

LET ME GO

I call on thee mother nature
From deep within my heart,
To wake me from my sleepy state
So that we can make a start.

Chorus
Oh mother nature I love thee so,
Open up my heart and let me go,
Let me go, let me go, I love thee so,
Let me go, let me go, let me go.

I call on thee to lift me up,
To show me far and wide,
The beauty of your realms
Reaching out from every side.

I call on thee to show me,
To appreciate what you can do,
I beg thee mother nature
If you will love me too.

Oh mother nature I love thee so,
Open up my heart and let me go,
Let me go, let me go, I love thee so,
Let me go, let me go, let me go,
Let me go, let me go, let me go,
Let me go, let me go, let me go.

our stay.

This little episode taught us to be aware that when we receive inspiration from spirit, to write it down, or in this case, record it. Our musical connection remained with us for a few weeks. One day while Marion was kneading the dough, she received inspiration for some music to 'Grant Me' and we lost no time in finding the recording machine. Feeling really inspired following this, she taped 'There Came a Tapping', and I added a chorus and we had another song. The climax for me came when she sang 'Take Me' to the music of 'Morning Has Broken'. It is not perfect but I introduced it to a large group at a workshop I was facilitating later in Scotland. For me it was a moving experience. I wept.

How this organisation is faring now I do not know, it was there for our experience. It taught us a great deal and opened the door for us to a wider world and we thank them for that. We met some beautiful people and some like us, have moved on from their experience. Some visitors to the organisation were members of yoga groups and cancer self-help groups and when they found out about our personal involvement in healing we were invited to visit them and facilitate workshops and give talks on its various aspects.

One of those dear souls we met was Gwyneth Poacher, one of the first two McMillan nurses in Wales. She is a natural healer, exuding vitality, a motivator and an inspirer, short in stature but big in heart. At that time, she founded a cancer self-help group in Porthcawl, South Wales and invited us to give a talk to the group. That was in 1987. Since then we visit Sandville Court Self-Help Group a few times every year to share our healing expertise with visitors at the drop-in centre.

The early years proved a struggle for Gwyneth, especially with the medical establishment, but with the help of many local organisations raised the money to purchase an old country club. The word cancer was removed from the title of the group to embrace all persons who had a potentially terminal or debilitating illness. This consequently opened up to the public and offers of help and charitable donations became more commonplace. Help came in refurbishing the building by staff from the gas board, fire service and local factories. The thirteen-bed centre has now expanded to incorporate a therapy complex, swimming pool, charity shop, hairdressing salon and education block. Complementary therapies are a central core to the provision of services including spiritual healing, aromatherapy, reflexology, massage, reiki, Bowen therapy, hypnotherapy, yoga, meditation and relaxation. Although the centre is primarily for the local community, the good news of this inspiring development has spread and Sandville receive many requests for respite care from many parts of the U.K.

For her efforts, Gwyneth has received many accolades, including a Heart of Gold Award from the Esther Rantzen Show and an M.B.E.

From our association with Gwyneth and Sandville we have learnt that where there is a will, there is a way and not to risk everything on one endeavour. Although Marion and I had it in mind to develop a healing centre, to keep it exclusively to healing would limit its potential and so we would allow it to unfold as a centre for spiritual teaching and psychic development.

Another centre that played a prominent role in our lives was Lendrick Lodge in the Trossachs, Scotland and the people that developed it as a yoga and holistic centre, Sarah and Tommy Mulvanny. Sarah instigated most of the visionary work, supported by husband Tommy the DIY estate manager. In its early development, we played a frequent role facilitating healing and awareness workshops and learnt a lot from Sarah about some of the pitfalls of running such a business and a charity. They have since retired to less active pursuits, handing over the Lodge to a younger enthusiastic team.

Our travels took us to other centres and establishments in the U.K. and by asking the relevant questions, formulated ideas on how we would run such a centre when it came to fruition.

In hindsight as a temporary expedient, we developed the concept of a healing centre at the Friends Meeting House in Stafford for one evening each week. The idea was each week to arrange for a guest speaker to talk about complementary health or psycho-spiritual subjects, socialise, and contact healing and meditation. After a slow start the word spread, maintaining a flow each week of two to three dozen enthusiasts maximising on occasions of more than fifty. As an Aquarian always anxious to devolve responsibility, I called upon the 'team' to engage upon a rota for making tea, chair for the evening and leader for the meditation. With a little arm-twisting encouragement, many realised they had hidden potential and an ability to speak

GRANT ME

God grant me the ability to Work
So that I may do it in your name,
And in so doing the nature of the effort
Has not made it all in vain.

God grant to me the Knowledge and the Wisdom
To understand the things within our store,
To decide how best that I may use them
To open up another door.

God grant me Love that I may have Compassion,
Charity, that I may give,
God help me share the gifts that I possess
In so doing that I may live.

God grant to me time for Worship
That I may thank you for this life,
To share with them the loving and the caring
Through times of happiness and strife.

God grant me Light to see the Truth
To make my reason much more sound,
So I may help to lay the paving
For a highway over stony ground.

publicly. Others after being encouraged by a particular therapy or discipline decided to progress along that pathway and later became qualified therapists.

After over two years at the helm, we knew the time was coming for us to move on but no one was willing to continue the course. It happens. Every ship needs a navigator but the centre had served its purpose, it charted a course for those that were ready to set sail and the experience certainly assisted our passage. For me personally it was an exercise keeping my ego in check by giving others permission to express and be themselves. As a lightworker I accepted the role, perhaps one who shines the light but not as a guru in the eastern tradition. Everyone is his or her own guru.

To have such leaders has been a necessity in the Piscean age. People in their ignorance needed role models or archetypes to follow and to teach them the way. Now in the age of Aquarius people are coming into a recognition of who they truly are, are becoming more self empowered, working with the concepts of brotherhood and unity towards common aims and objectives of peace, love and humanity. Indeed, there will always be a need for someone to carry the mantle of responsibility, but more in the role of a facilitator.

Facilitators can make a passage easy or they can make a passage possible and sometimes there is a necessity to press buttons to bring about a release with uncomfortable results and surfacing of issues.

If a person or group reacts against you then it may be of two things. That there is an attitudinal problem with you or that there is a group dynamic that has not been resolved. If you have no axe to grind with the individuals concerned, your manner is used to push buttons to release energies that were dormant and needed expression. The dynamics of the group or person have not moved far enough forward out of their safe environment.

There is no progress unless two sides of the coin can show itself. It is then on edge and can move forward.

Because we felt so passionate about healing, we wanted to share it and help others to tune into their own source and spent evenings, weekends and holidays working to itineraries in different parts of the

UK. Starting with women's institute meetings, we followed through working with many self-help groups in areas of cancer, multiple sclerosis and mental health. We were helping sufferers to take some responsibility for their well-being, by doing something simple. Our diversions also took us into Her Majesty's detention centres, not permanently, but for health fairs organized by the prison authorities.

At first, our exhibition stand was for healing but we were not surprisingly, passed by in favour of interest in drug and sex education. That changed when we altered our display to stress management. They came in their droves. In the course of the day, Marion and I would be working on over one hundred staff and inmates, giving and sharing a few minutes with each and giving a lasting experience and hopefully, touching their soul at a deeper level.

Chapter 7

Peacehaven – Beginnings

Be still and know,
that I am your refuge in the corners of your mind,
in the moment of despair there I will be your find;
through times of sorrow with many things to cure,
I am your strength with a love to endure.

On reaching the magic milestone of fifty, I accepted the opportunity of early retirement and redundancy from my work as a local government officer in the engineering department. I did not need any encouragement; in fact, over the previous eighteen months I had watched my older colleagues clap their hands with joy whilst I went green at the gills. I knew that it would happen one day for me to fulfil that prediction, though I did not know quite how. After checking our finances, agreeing our objectives I secured the best birthday present possible. It was not just the financial incentive but also the freedom to fulfil my/our destiny.

We did not go tearing off immediately searching for the place that was supposed to be waiting for us. Our house went on the market and we waited. And waited. And waited. Those of you who want to move on, know exactly how that feels. It was not until three years later about Easter '97 that we at last had an offer we could not refuse, but there was no hurry for us to move out. The house-price boom also blessed us in the 1980's, which quadrupled the price, which subsequently helped us to purchase the place we were looking for.

Searching for a needle in a haystack was something else. All I knew was that haystack was in the Welsh Marches or just beyond, I had a pull, a longing towards Wales. The hills and mountains have always held a longing for me; it was though I was entranced by a spell from bygone days. Who knows, perhaps past-life memories.

Our search started in the Forest of Dean Gloucestershire, an area we felt that time had forgot, and over a three year period we slowly made our way northwards through the placidity of Herefordshire, the undulations of Shropshire and into the gentle rolling hills of Powys. In our quest, we had travelled into some lovely and unspoilt areas of the U.K., appreciating some beautiful parts that we may never have seen had we gone straight to Montgomeryshire. We were grateful for that.

On the other hand, I was pulling my hair out. I wanted action; now, yesterday. Frustration, desperation and Marion were my bed-partners, not that she is in the same mould, but I was glad she was there to keep my sanity. I just wanted to get on with the job I came here to do although in my heart I knew the outworking of destiny would reveal itself at the right time. Clichés: I had heard them all, from every quarter, from all our friends and from spirit until I was sick of them. I knew we would find the place we were looking for but I wanted it now. It got to a stage in my irreverence that I said to him, it, the management, whoever you are, 'If you don't get your bloody finger out, I'm going to jack everything'. In my heart, I knew I would not, but it made me feel better. Of course, the management knew that too. If it were possible, I could imagine the laughter all around me. If you want to make God laugh, tell Him your plans.

As part of my quest, I realised that other doors were opening for me.

A few years earlier our friend Kim Hughes, with whom we did a lot of personal energy work with the assistance of her guides, introduced me to the concept of earth energies. With her help, I learnt how to tune in to the energies around us. All it really needs is for someone to take you through different energies emanating from the earth. Once you become aware, you can try it yourself and have someone like Kim around who can confirm your discovery. All of us have so many latent gifts or talents; it just needs us to be open to the possibility and for someone to show or assist us on the way. Kim first confirmed my openness to earth energies at Chalice Well, Glastonbury. If you feel or sense something different get someone to tune in and perhaps experience what you are sensing to confirm you are not in cuckoo land. It allows you to progress forwards and gain more confidence.

On one of our frequent visits to the Forest of Dean, we met up with an old friend Jay who also is very sensitive and relies very much on her intuitive guidance. As we drove along a country lane, I felt a distinct change in the energy. I commented to Jay 'Did you feel that'? She confirmed and we all had an attack of goose bumps. I turned the car and slowed down over the spot and there it was again. Marion was elated as she also could feel the difference. We did not stay to try to sense the reason for the energy change, but on a later visit to the area, I felt a strong desire to stop at a three-way country crossroads. I walked the area and felt a pull to a triangular grass island. As I stood still and opened myself up with a little invocation to the earth, I felt a rush of energy flow up, tingling throughout my body. I did not know particularly why I was attracted to that location but it was sufficient to know that I was a channel of some sort to release that earth energy.

A few other occasions I received directions intuitively, which I believed was to be the location of our future home but it again turned out that I was to be a channel for earth healing.

Early one morning whilst meditating in bed, I asked for directions as to where we should go house hunting. A very clear message echoed through my mind, 'Thirty miles south and twenty miles west'. I had not a clue where it was until a map revealed an area southwest of Kidderminster. Marion drove, I navigated with intuition, 'Next right, left, right again, etc., take the next right and we are there'. Well we were at the entrance to a disused quarry. I was just about to vent my abuse at the universe, then I realised I was here to do some earth healing. I trundled up the steep incline and tuned in to a location to do my party piece forming a bridge and inviting healing energies to heal this scarred land. Just as I completed my invocation, a jet flew out of nowhere rising parallel to the incline and nearly took my eardrums apart. Momentarily I could see the pilot smiling 'Gotcha'. I was conned again.

After that episode, I remained open to all possibilities. Whenever I received specific directions, I knew it was for earth healing. On another occasion, armed with directions we ended up near the Wyre Forest, Worcestershire. I left the car, walked across a field, and ventured deep into a coniferous wood. Eventually the sound of machinery meandered through the trees together with the crashing fall of the sentinels of our earth. I found a location of the noise, opened up and requested healing for the area.

Therefore, while I was milling around the country being usefully employed by spirit, it did not help to temper my impatience.

Naturally, we asked Ruth if she could tune in on our behalf. She could not help with specifics either, except that it was not far from a castle and that human vibrations relating to the place go back a long way. September also would be a month of change and we would go somewhere first for a rest period but it would all happen very quickly. It did not sound much but we found later that it was pretty well on the mark, except that we did not know which September.

The rolling hills of Montgomeryshire were pulling us ever closer. We often frequented the estate agents at Welshpool and the shire towns, and gave scrutiny to the literature we collected. Our prospective purchaser indicated that she would like to move in during the school holidays so we were getting desperate.

On one of our visits, we decided to stay over at a Churchstoke farm for bed and breakfast and replenished ourselves at a local hostelry. I enquired from the barmaid about any property for short term let and she suggested we visit a local lass Lee. Well Lee was something else. As soon as we walked down the driveway to her cottage she and her partner had renovated, and told of our desperate dilemma, she welcomed us with open arms. Lee is one of those people you could not miss - big in stature - to accommodate big heart. She had done most things in life and never said no to a challenge, so she said to leave it with her, she would find us somewhere to park ourselves, as a temporary measure.

We slept a little easier that night and after a few more house visits the next day made our way home.

A call from our solicitor greeted our arrival with a request for vacation on 1st August. Fortunately we had packed most our possessions away in boxes and had been that way for several weeks but we were still up to the early hours scampering away like little mice. Lee rang the next day and she had secured a let on the property adjacent to hers at a very modest rent. It was a three-bed dormer bungalow with converted garage had apparently been up for sale for several months - and did we need that extra space!

We said our farewells to Staffordshire on 1st August and a special thank you to our house that had served us well for thirteen years, to all the energies that had come to visit us and wished it well in its retirement.

Churchstoke provided a rest period of sorts; at least we did not have the hassle of travelling great distances looking for property. On one of our earlier excursions to the estate agents, we collected details of two properties that were up for auction. The first was 'Peace Office', a six-acre smallholding with corrugated metal barns and the second was another two-acre farm at Ratlinghope in Shropshire. I was attracted to Ratlinghope mainly because of its local stone appearance and had immediate potential for development but Marion fancied 'Peace Office'.

I really could not work up a lot of enthusiasm, we had been chasing around for three years, despairing, plus the guide price of Peace Office was artificially low to create interest and my estimate of its value was far in excess of what we could afford. So a few days before the auction on 11th August at the end of my tether I surrendered my desires to the universe, willing to accept whatever comes.

Lee came with us to the auction and that was another blessing. On hearing of our interest, some farmers ushered us to sit in front of the auctioneer. It was as well because I could not understand a word. When the figure reached the guide price and just as the hammer was about to go down, Lee waved her hand and then I quickly took over. We finally secured the property for just above the guide price and we could afford it with some cash to spare.

Marion and I then went into a state of shock. After all, that searching, despairing, moaning, and grumping (from me) we had finally come to the end of this phase of our journey. Feeling completely sapped of all energy we could barely write the cheque but we were congratulated by members of the local farming community. Since our interest was not at full throttle, I had not even bothered contacting our solicitor or the building society to have the money available. We were down to lose quite some interest without giving withdrawal notice but after a wonderful discussion with the manager, the interest was reinstated, together with an offer of solicitor's fees for being good customers.

As predicted, it all happened so quickly, in the space of three weeks. Finally we were interred on the autumn equinox in Peace Office four miles from Powys Castle, which we renamed 'Peacehaven'.

Apart from the financial benefits, we received in the sale and the tremendous help from Lee there were a number of other pointers that indirectly and unconsciously led us to 'Peacehaven'.

When one is on the lookout for a potential house/home there are certain essential criteria that one needs, for instance three bedrooms, a large garden, double glazing, etc. Well we had a few and we added to them as the months dragged by. To summarise we put them under the heading:

Wouldn't it be nice if.......

we had at least an acre, which grew to six at the end of our search
the house is in the centre of the property
the property is accessible, preferably off a B-road
the house is back from the road
we had barns that could be converted for a meeting room and workshops
there was a room for healing
there was an extra room for meditation / counselling / waiting area ˙
there were trees around the property
there was running water i.e. a stream or river
there was a north facing kitchen (Marion likes a cool kitchen when baking)

We did not ask for much, actually very little. We just expressed 'wouldn't it be nice if....'and it did not occur to us until we visited Peacehaven on the afternoon of the auction that all these 'if only' things were there. It was as if someone upstairs was listening to every word, writing it down and laughing their socks off. There were also two other little additions to our list. I was always ripping my shirtsleeves on door handles and I vowed that when we moved I would replace all handles with knobs, so what did we have waiting for us? We also fell in love with a dark red flowering currant on our travels, and what was flowering in our garden the following spring?

There have been many pleasant discoveries since we came to stay here. We have been so busy with household creativity, but we still take time to stand still and marvel at the works of nature, of life and the creative essence that unifies everything and we give thanks for the many blessings that have come our way.

WHERE ARE YOU?

Many houses there are standing
In honour of his name,
Built of bricks and mortar
Each playing a different game.
In his universe are many mansions
Each a facet of his being,
They are all a part of him
All knowing, all loving and all seeing.
It is good to come in unison
And send to him your praise,
But know that he is everywhere
In many different ways.
You can praise him while you toil
As you walk along the street,
You can offer up a humble prayer
For every one you meet.
You need only smile a little
Express the love within your soul,
Let it shine through glistening eye
And know you have scored a goal.
The essence of God is everywhere
In every leaf and tree,
In every living creature
He has shared with us for free.
God works wonders with his life-forms
Bringing comfort, beauty and cheer,
But most of all in the garden
You will find he is always near.

PEACEHAVEN
Courtesy of Brynmor Shaw

Gratitude is an expression of love. Your whole lives should be one of gratitude because of the privilege you have of experiencing a life in the physical dimension. It provides you with the greatest opportunities for the growth of your soul, through the experience of good and bad, positive and negative, light and dark. You have complete freedom of choice to determine your teachings, to learn, to grow in wisdom through the balance of experience. In consideration of what each experience in your life has taught you from a higher perspective or understanding is a great gift and brings with it much wisdom and for this you should express your gratitude.

Life is an opportunity to express love in diverse ways, with gratitude to the great source of love, to the many other little sources around you and not forgetting the little source within.

CHAPTER 8

Into The Stillness

Be still and know,
I am that which you seek that all evading peace,
you will find me in the stillness, once found, will never cease.
I am found in all things, if you would but try to begin
to be still and full of awareness and then you will take me in.

WHAT IS MEDITATION?

According to some orientations or belief persuasions, meditation is evil.

In truth, humans have been meditating since time began. Dictionaries define meditation as to consider thoughtfully, study, concentrate, focus, reflect, and deliberate to name but a few synonyms. These definitions will tell us that all of us have meditated at some time or another. All it means is being still and to take it a little further, appreciating that moment of being in the here and now.

Stagnation may also a great teaching because it can provide an opportunity for great growth and understanding. As a seed may sometimes be frozen before it is sown, the shock of raising its surrounding temperature will spring it to life. There are so many who feel that they are frozen, that they are in the ice of stagnation. The secret of melting the frosty thoughts of the ice ego you have created is through your own inner awareness - of being aware in this moment of time of who and what you are. This will indeed light your fire and the iceberg you have created will melt from within.

In a sense, you are like blocks of ice, solidified in form and the light you need is to transform you first into water of the fourth dimension, where you are more fluid and open in your outlook and more flexible. Then with more light, you will evaporate becoming an ocean of mist - all knowing, expansive, accessible to everything. This is the space where you can transform to with the light that you bring to yourself.

Stagnation as you would have it is staying where you are, of not moving, not learning, not doing, of making no apparent progress. It has also another side that may lead you into a more positive form of progress, and may take you into the stillness and the quiet waters of meditation if you would but begin to focus your thoughts on being still. Winter is a period of apparent stagnation when all lies dormant and asleep but in that quiet, it may be used as a period of reflection and introspection of your life and how it has unfolded.

WHY MEDITATE?

There are diverse reasons why people choose to meditate, each one of them a personal reason or experience. So let us look at some of these objectives.

Improves Health and Relieves Stress.

Science has shown us that when we are in a meditative or alpha state endorphins are released into our body, which gives a boost to our immune system, so on that prognosis, if we meditate all the time we should be in a state of continual well being. Unfortunately, being in that state will not feed our stomachs, get our jobs done or pay our bills.

On the other hand, we can use the power of visualisation or imagery to assist the body, mind and emotions to heal themselves. Apart from physical illnesses, various visualisations may help overcome addictions, insomnia and depression, anxiety, releasing fears, and calming the mind.

Relaxation

To help calm the body and bring it to rest, we may adopt a sequence of tensing the muscles and letting them relax. By focussing your attention on a particular part of the body, holding your attention there whilst tensing that area and letting it suddenly relax, will allow the tension being held there to drain away. You can also include breathing exercises while tensioning the muscles; visualise the breath going to the area of the tension and releasing the tension on the outbreath, should assist in releasing the blocked or stagnant energy from within the muscles.

Connects with Inner Resources and Self Development

Most of us go through life, rushing around trying to get things done, meeting schedules and trying to do things the way we want or the way that society demands of us. Rather than a 'human doing', if we can consider ourselves as a 'spiritual being' we are able to look at life from an entirely different perspective. As a spirit, we have the ability to be a natural embodiment of love, compassion, freedom and creativity.

By spending time in constructive meditation, by being still, we can allow our whole world to open up in as natural a way as possible. So much guidance is available intuitively and all we have to do is ask. By focussing on your question or scenario and then leaving yourself open for answers is an important key, instead of keeping crossing those bridges and wearing out your shoe leather. The answers may not always be immediately apparent or they may come later when you least expect it but they will be there, sometimes in symbolic form like those you may receive in dream state. In learning to trust these responses, you develop your gut response or intuition. As you learn to work more with your intuition, know that it is your wise councillor; you trust it even more and it subsequently enhances your positive attitudes towards life and yourself as an esteemed, worthy and confident being.

Every being is naturally creative. Each of us has an ability to create and many of us do so in the most natural way possible by reproduction, but there are so many other limitless ways in which we can be productive that can bring so much joy and happiness and open up lonely hearts. Stepping into the silence and asking how you may be more creative may give the answers, again when it is more appropriate for you to receive. It is no good wanting to express your innermost desires and feelings if you do not give yourself the time and space to allow that creativity to unfold in as natural a way as possible.

Meditation allows space for introspection. It enables you to look at where you are, what your goals are in life and what you are able to do to achieve those goals if that is the pathway you are supposed to be following at this time. By practice, you will be able to step outside of yourself and look at your situation with detachment, peace and great compassion, to give yourself guidance from the depth of your soul.

Increases Awareness

Many of us go through life oblivious and insensitive to the beauty that surrounds us, in particular the energy that expresses that beauty.

There are times when all should be at peace and all should be at peace at all times. These are the quiet times when you would look into the pit of darkness, whereby it becomes a portal to other frequencies of vibration, allowing you to unlock the doors that limit your consciousness.

Take this time to concentrate on creations of beauty within your existence, feel the energies of what you perceive them to be. Use this time as an extension to that which you set apart in your daily existence and being aware of the energies around you. In this quiet time you are developing your sensitivity into realising that you are unlimited. You have just forgotten how, you have just become desensitised by the bustle of your physical experience. Be patient with your concentration and contemplations and do not despair.

Take the time to investigate and contemplate the natural world and discover that this world also is part of other vibrations. There are so many vibrations all operating at the same time but at different frequencies, but it is possible through the practice of meditation, of being still, to tune into these frequencies. It is like opening the door of your consciousness and stepping into a room that has no walls. It is possible for all to sense these vibrations. In learning to sense, it is possible to become at one with these energies, which is all that you are required to do at this point in your evolution.

All are striving, perhaps unconsciously, for that at-oneness with all creation and what better place to contemplate that than in your own garden, or a walk in awareness of your natural surroundings, or sensing a plant or a pebble beneath your feet.

You have the keys of your physical senses to give you the freedom from limitation. Stretch your senses in the quiet time increase their frequencies and you will surely find your world is but a grain of sand on a limitless beach suffused in the sunlight of creation.

Contact with Other Realities

One of the greatest benefits of meditation is going within and contacting our own spiritual essence, listening to the still small voice of our soul. Here is the key to our divinity, which will help us remember who we are and what we are capable of being.

Being still, open and developing the art of being receptive, will make connections with other realities and dimensions, of which there are many. We all have guidance throughout our lives; the physical, through the people with whom we come into contact and the spiritual, the discarnate beings in lighter and finer dimensions or vibrations than the physical. They may also be angelic, of a much finer vibration. They are all there to assist our passage through life if we ask for it, to help us awaken to our true nature and purpose in life.

WHEN TO MEDITATE

As mentioned earlier, most of us meditate unconsciously at various times throughout the day, so you can meditate anytime, anywhere by any method that you choose.

If possible, allow yourself to be comfortable, not so that you will fall asleep, but also so that you are free from pain and discomfort. Even if you manage to snatch three minutes at a time (in the loo) it is worth it although at least a twenty-minute session is more desirable.

The main problem that many experience when meditating is self-discipline, actually setting aside the time on your own and consciously moving into a meditative state. It is far easier when meditating in the group situation, you know you have a set time and place and if individual motives are of the right order, a harmony develops within the group with a lifting of energy levels.

True meditation in fact begins when you are unaware of it, being totally absorbed in the present moment.

WAYS TO MEDITATE

A mediation ritual may be performed in a number of ways and for convenience, are categorised as follows:

- **Visual**

  This entails focussing on a candle flame, crystal or some other object in front of you or in your mind's eye.

  Those that have difficulty using their imagination will find it easier to have their eyes open initially and closing them for short periods, maintaining the image in their mind's eye.

  With the eyes closed, the participant uses a visualisation involving some sort of familiar journey, perhaps to somewhere special.

- **Auditory**

  Listening to recorded music or a guided visualisation will maintain a focussed connection.

  By continually repeating a mantra, or a positive word such as love or peace this has the effect of blotting out the mind chatter that is so prevalent in meditation.

  Listening to the rhythm of breathing focuses continual attention of the journey of the in and out breath.

- **Sensory**

  Feeling the breath as it enters the nostril and travels to the lungs and feeling the exhalation. Awareness of the breath is an inner transformative process. It takes you into your own space away from thinking. Being conscious of breathing brings you into the present moment.

  Working with rosary or prayer beads, or holding a crystal or other tangible object enables a constant attention to feeling.

- **Movement**

  Some people find it considerably difficult to sit still for any length of time and it is perfectly acceptable to choose to meditate whilst on the move. Walking or gardening at the same time being continually aware and appreciative of the detail of your surroundings will fulfil this purpose, as will the practise of tai chi, chi kung or other routine involving gentle movement.

Which way you meditate is down to personal preference and any combination of methods may be used at any one time.

Meditation Procedure

There is no right way to meditate, just the way that suits you using your own regime.

As a standard to start with, you may adopt the following procedure:

- Sit comfortably and adjust your posture for comfort. Do not cross your legs and rest your hands on your lap to maintain the energy flow around your body. Fingers may be intertwined or touching.

- Offer up a prayer stating your openness to receive and ask for protection. (see appendix) Requesting protection does not necessarily mean that something undesirable will or may happen. It means that if an immature student who has also some psychic ability opens up too readily then they may attract undesirable energies. In any event, the group leader should be able to control the situation.

- Relax the body fully and release any tensions by using the breath and directing it into the tensed area and releasing tensions with the exhalation.

- Breathe down a ray of golden light from the universe to enter the crown of your head. You may link the source of this light to God, your higher self or some other deified being depending on your particular belief system. Fill your body up with this light down to your feet and visualise your body opening up to this energy. This is accomplished by opening up the seven main energy centres or chakras in the body and symbolically they may be represented by flower buds opening to full flower.

- Allow the light to flow out from your body, into the space around you and from your feet into the earth.

- Focus on the heart, see it glow and send a ray of golden light up to the third eye to illumine the mind. Concentrate on the third eye and see it as a white screen.

- Be aware of that screen together with the pictures or symbols that may appear and of energies and feelings that may come to you. Do not expect or anticipate. Be patient and persevere.

- On completion of the session, close down your chakras and ground yourself by visualising one of the following:
  o standing in running water or
  o growing roots from your feet into the earth or
  o being surrounded in a bubble of golden light or
  o place a gold cross in a circle over each chakra

- Offer up a prayer of gratitude.

- Acknowledge your experiences by discussing them with the group or write them down in a journal.

Visualisation

Probably the most used meditative tool, it carries with it enormous power as it is used by the mind to heal the body and relieve stress. In using the imagination with positive intention, we can improve our well-being. Imagination creates thoughts and ideas into a picture or scenario, which is then activated to produce a positive outcome.

General Procedure

Key points to remember when using visualisation techniques as an aid to healing and health improvement are as follows:

- Relax
- See the illness objectively and be specific
- See the agents of disease as weak and disorganised
- See it under control by medication and body defences

- Feel in the body what the mind is seeing
- Speak to the dis-ease and try to ascertain why it is there
- See the agents of healing as strong and vigorous
- Thank it, forgive it and yourself, *love it to bits* and let it go
- See a restoration to perfect health – conviction helps
- It is useful to understand the anatomy of the problem and the causes of symptoms in order to help customise intentions through visualisations

Every time you make way for the energy of life to flow through you, you will know that it will change you for further development. The accelerated changes with you and others are very much dependent on consciously absorbing the life force with the breath and bringing that light through your whole body and the space of your energy field.

Within the atmosphere are particles of energy that your bodies require to make the necessary evolutionary changes. This energy is affecting your energy fields and reacting on your bodies and may cause physical disturbances and discomfort. By processing the energy through the breath and breathing it through your energy centres, the physical body will be able to cope more adequately with these disturbances. In allowing that energy to come from within out instead of outside in, then you are making a conscious acceptance of what your body needs and adaptation will be easier.

Many exercise the breathing in of the light, which will assist in the transformation to become light beings, but the particles of energy are a little more than that. To explain more it is suggested that you perform the following visualisation with regularity.

Visualise the light above your head and breathe that light down through the alpha, crown, brow, etc chakras, through the omega and down into the earth. Visualise yourself in a column of light from the source of the universe into the centre of the earth. Allow the light to flow, from your open chakras into the energy field around you.

Imagine now that your beam of light is condensing into minute particles, like stardust containing myriads of colours over your physical body. There are large amounts of gold, silver, opal and pearl particles as well as other colours of the spectrum. Feel that these colours bring with them vitality, richness and love that is a gift from the creative essence and with that love you begin to feel that your heart and body opens in a total act of surrender as you accept this blessing. Allow your body to absorb the stardust and to settle within your being. Enfold yourself around these minute starseeds and with the love given to you, allow them to grow into beautiful flowers within, flowers of love, truth, wisdom, grace and divine will.

As you engage in your peace now, know that you will share that peace and truth and touch many others in the times of change.

For further meditations, see Appendix 2

CHAPTER 9

The Face Of Healing

Be still and know,
when my love stirs from deep within it opens up a door,
allowing all your precious gifts to burst forth from within your store.
Your gifts are like the flowers, allow their fruits to be
pluck them, give them freely, for all humanity.

As I mentioned earlier my work with healing has been my own unique experience. I did ask for the purpose of my life to become manifest and it did, in no mean measure. I was ready and allowed my box to open, allowing my light to shine. As I consumed each morsel of experience, I needed more sustenance and more understandings came from within, which in turn led on to more other fruits I had to digest. Even after over twenty-five years of healing there are still pills I have to swallow in my personal development.

There were very few instructions and assistance available in the early years, but I believe my experience was a good teacher and served me well when it came to delivering talks to groups coming from different backgrounds. We collected information based on their questions, what the audiences wanted to know about aspects of healing that surfaced through my own experience, observations and reasoning.

WHAT IS HEALING?

Healing has many faces, which has suited the make-up of man for thousands of years. Most indigenous races, groups, sects and religions realised that this energy could be directed or channelled and was related to and part of the essence of the source of all being. Where there was disharmony within the physical body, it was generally considered that the personality of that being was disassociating itself from its own soul essence. Over many hundreds of years healing, it was called by many names but it all came under the umberellic term of energy healing.

Healing is the transference of energy from one sentient being to another (and may include all kingdoms of matter) in which the recipient derives some benefit from the experience. In simple terms, this energy said to be the life force, which flows throughout the universe and is interchangeable with all matter. This definition also fits the theory of quantum physics that all matter is energy and all living organisms have an energy field. At this time scientific methods have not proved the efficacy of healing and as such healing is unrecognised by science, yet there is plenty of anecdotal evidence available. Pick up any healers autobiographies and you will find ample stories of effective 'cures'.

By learning to channel and attune to this life force, it is possible to heal. Many choose to use God as being the ultimate source of this energy, universal energy, Christ, Mohammed or other religious deities, the higher self, or angels. Some choose to love unconditionally and that is sufficient to channel this healing energy. This is why so many who have an abundance of love energy and personal vitality are natural healers.

There are a number of common labels or techniques in use when referring to healing and the most commonly used has been *faith healing* or the *laying on of hands*. Over the centuries, the churches have used these labels since they had the monopoly of healing, at the same time implying that you had to have faith to become well. When the healings did not occur, the sinners were blamed, which did not help their self-esteem or faith.

An alternative expression that was quite popular with the advent of spiritualism was and still is *spiritual healing*, because guides and angels through their physical mediums channelled the healing. It was natural therefore to add spiritual to healing. Healers now tend to interpret spiritual as another name for the universal energy rather than have any religious connotations.

Healing means to make better, to make whole, repair or restore balance. Healing is the use of energy specifically to bring about change for the good, that is, with good intention.

Good intention may be equated to God intervention and since all are an aspect of God you are intervening as the god that you are. God is everything and nothing. It, she, he has no desires or wants. It is the intentional energy that humans add to this energy that defines what God is and is not.

You are the essence of the natural energy of the universe. You are part of it. So what makes this energy 'spiritual'?

To be spiritual is to be or have high or good intentions. It is being on and using the intention of a love vibration. The term 'spiritual' also corners the energy as coming from the spiritual dimensions or other realities which indeed it does, but it also comes from the earth, nature and from within, sometimes with equal and positive results.

So we have vibrational, intentional, energy, balance, spiritual, trance, earth, natural, psychic, reality, higher-dimensional, universal, faith, cellular as adjuncts to healing in an attempt to redefine its origins or purpose. Healing is all these things and much more.

How healing is channelled is very much a personal conviction. It is not just what you tune into that gets results but the power of your own intention together with the vibration of love that you wish to share that produces positive results.

Labels are a way of introducing limitation of saying what is. Since God is something that is not, nothing, in that it has no limitations, healing may also be called unlimited healing. But God is the essence of life, of the universe, God is the essence of healing – essential healing.

Is it essential to quantify or qualify the source from which it originated? It is all healing. Once the energy or the way you deliver is qualified, people will have a preconception of what it is and react accordingly, but by generalising, healing will be all things to all people.

In its broader context the term spiritual may be applied referring to a higher vibration of energy, which it is, but will take a little longer to be accepted the way it is intended.

In 1972 Dolores Krieger and Doris Kunz in the USA developed another system of healing referred to as therapeutic touch, which entailed working on the energy field using a series of hand movements a few centimetres from the body and is very similar to the way in which some spiritual healers work when they channel healing.

Some people have a natural ability to make others better using their own psychic healing or magnetic healing. They seem to have an abundance of this life force and by shear act of will or intention can bring about a positive change in someone's health. In the early days of my apprenticeship, I tried this a few times and consequently felt much

TAKE ME

Open my eyes Lord to see your ways
To shorten the nights and lengthen the days,
Take my eyes to see their plight
When hope is gone – no more to fight.

Take my tongue Lord to speak your voice
To show them all of their choice,
Through pain and suffering and many a care
To make it easier, a cross to bear.

Take my hands Lord to ease the pain
And show them all it's not in vain,
Opening their hearts with the feeling
Of the warmth of your love and your healing.

To you my Lord I wholly surrender
Instruct me your way to be a mender,
To gather the pieces of a mind scattered
By hurt and suffering, worn and battered.

Let me search Lord and help me find
The dying remnants of a broken mind,
And through me you can do what is willed
Then two people will be fulfilled.

depleted and tired.

Reiki healing is a system of healing developed out of Japan based on using universal energy. It is much the same as spiritual healing apart from having a number of set moves and attuning to symbols at different stages of development. Some practitioners maintain there is no difference in the channelling of the life force or universal energy as with spiritual healing. Having discussed channelling healing energy with a number of Reiki practitioners, there essentially appears to be very little difference in the two methods.

Surprisingly on a number of occasions as a preliminary discourse with patients, I have asked if they have had healing before and received a negative response. I also asked if they have received Reiki and they replied positively. It shows clearly the lack of understanding on behalf of the public and even more so the lack of education by the healing movement.

Many healers would argue there is no such thing as a *quick fix*. It is possible when the time is right and the recipient is open and ready at a soul level for a healing to occur then it may only take as much as a minute to effect a cure. There have been instances on our journey where a 'quick fix' has provided the necessary dispersal of pain.

The aim of any act of healing should be to improve the quality of life but unfortunately, because of man's limited perspectives of health issues there has been a tendency to think in terms of curing the physical body. Because symptoms may remain after a healing session with its apparent lack of effectiveness the conclusion is that it has not worked. In fact, healing occurs at other levels than physical; it may affect us emotionally, mentally or spiritually. If pain persists, it may not mean that a complete healing has occurred, since the pain may be the result of an emotional trauma or stress, which needs attention.

All is energy. Matter is energy, light is energy and the highest vibration of all, love is energy. Each frequency of a higher vibration is able to change and transform energy of a lower vibration if it is in accordance with the will of that lower vibration. Yet those lower vibrations are also able to teach the higher vibrations of their experience. By this interaction, each vibration is able to assist another. This is how we help each other from our respective perspectives of vibration. Much is learned from your teachings and assistance may be given in changing your situation at your request and if it is in the interest for your greatest good.

Because you have that power, you possess those higher vibrations of consciousness you are able to create. You do create from the thought patterns you allow to become manifest, be it unconsciously. You can create atmospheres from energy and by being in a particular state of mind you are able to influence the lives of others. By allowing these thoughts around you in abundance, you create your own reality.

This is how you create your own diseases and illnesses, from your negative states of mind. By creating and absorbing negative thought patterns into your emotional body, you are able to absorb those patterns into your physical energy system and bring about an imbalance, through the existence of disease or injury. With that manifestation comes the pain. Your malfunction is trying to tell you that there is an imbalance in your physical body - that there is something wrong. Pain will teach you not only that there is imbalance but its location also will indicate the factors and states of mind contributing to the imbalance. Learn also of those parts of the body that relate to your energy system, their synchronicity, so pain, although a product of lower vibratory thought, can teach you much.

Pain endeavours to bring balance, to provide the means to un-create that which you have created. Pain is not your master but a master teacher to help you become a master of matter.

Raise your vibrations to an even higher level and connect to that part of you that holds no negative thoughts, only love, and you will no longer need pain, the teacher, because there is no imbalance in your being.

WHAT ABOUT QUALIFICATIONS?

Since the use of complementary and alternative medicines (CAM) has become widespread in the U.K. and is increasing across the developed world, the House of Lords published a report in November 2000 to consider significant issues relating to complementary and alternative medicine.

The issues considered were whether:

- good structures of regulation are in place to protect the public
- research is being carried for an accumulation of evidence

- adequate information sources are available
- the practitioners training is adequate
- the prospects for NHS provision of the treatments

All therapies considered were categorised into groups. Healing was included in the group which contains those therapies which are most often used to complement conventional medicine and do not purport to embrace diagnostic skills. The committee were also satisfied that many therapies in this group give help and comfort to many patients when used in a complementary sense even though most of them lack a firm scientific base

This 141-page report considers evidence submissions from many sources covering topics of patient satisfaction, evidence for efficacy, regulation, professional training and education, research and development, information and delivery.

Summary of recommendations pertinent to healing

- Therapies which assist in the area of relaxation and stress management (the healing group), should control their claims according to the evidence available to them.
- If a therapy does gain a critical mass of evidence to support its efficacy, then the *NHS* and the medical profession should ensure that the public has access to it and its potential benefits.
- Each of the therapies should organise themselves under a single professional body for each therapy. These bodies should promote themselves so that the public and healthcare professionals who access these therapies are aware of them. Patients could then have a point of reference for standards, and with protection against the risk of poorly trained practitioners.
- CAM therapists should collaborate more closely, especially on developing reliable public information sources.
- All CAM training courses should become more standardised and be accredited and validated by the appropriate professional bodies.
- The Department of Health should make information on CAM available through NHS Direct. The information should contain not only contact details of the relevant bodies and a list of NHS

provision of CAM in each local area, but also some guidance to help patients (and their doctors) evaluate different CAM therapies.

- CAM regulatory bodies remind their members of the laws concerning false claims in advertisements and take disciplinary action against anyone who breaks them
- There should be more integration between CAM and conventional medicine. CAM practitioners and GPs should keep an open mind about each other's ability to help their patients, to make patients feel comfortable about integrating their health care provision and to exchange information about treatment programmes.

The government responded in March 2001 and was supportive of this document and its recommendations.

A reaction of this report from many healing organisations is that it seems fair and seeks to determine a base for 'professionalism' and public safety. For public and therapists to feel happy with the outcomes, education, training, research and development are key issues that should be considered. It also seems that Healing no longer has to justify itself on a hard scientific basis and could be more universally adopted as a therapy with correct regulation and training.

In the early years of my journey as a healer I was a freelance, exploring and sharing healing, not wanting to join an organisation that would regulate what I should and should not do. That is until others migrated towards me for 'training', I then became consciously aware of their needs to feel the security of a qualification of competence. For some people and establishments a certified piece of paper speaks reams. I know how qualifications helped my career prospects so I joined one such organisation. U-turning my ideas and concepts, not by coercion, but because I feel for healing to be fully accepted and utilised, it must conform to what the public desire of it, not to have a sense of mystery about it, but to express that love by going with the flow.

Healing is not only a 'gift'. It is a right. A gift implies an award to an individual or group because they have earned it in some way. Healing is an aspect of that life force that pervades throughout the universe, like a by-product or reaction that utilises that life-force in a particular way. That life force flows through every thing. We are an aspect of that force. Through our development and awareness as sentient beings, we are able to harness and use that energy in diverse ways. Healing is one of them.

Many of those who practice healing feel that it is a gift and developed intuitively, so why should they undergo the rigours of an academic curriculum together with training with a bone fide healer. Since the mid 1950's, healers such as Harry Edwards have tried to establish credibility with the medical fraternity and scientific establishment, but because there has been no scientific basis for a cure, healing has had little acceptance. Now that barrier is beginning to be lifted there remains the concern for public safety (and for protection of the therapist/healer).

This really means that if anyone wishes to practice healing in the public domain, they should be suitably qualified and registered. This does not mean that those who have a 'gift' cannot use it in a private capacity amongst family and friends.

Beside the various training curriculum's instigated by the various healing organisations and supported and accredited by UK Healers, there are however a number of 'qualities' a potential healer should take on board when channelling healing energy.

By far one of the most demanding necessities required of a healer, indeed of anyone working in the caring professions is that of **detachment**. Where there is a desire to help others there is always the possibility of taking on and getting involved in their stuff. Once you start getting emotionally involved with your client, for instance being overly sympathetic, then your love has strings attached and love that has strings is not unconditional. Be empathetic and feel their trauma, maybe even understand it if you have been there but keep sympathy to a minimum.

Detachment is one of the most difficult issues that you face in your lifetimes. Your desires lock you into another's reality with your emotional hooks that it becomes difficult to pull away without causing hurt to yourself or the other party.

You do not have to be sponges for all the garbage comes your way. There are ways in which you can detach yourselves from this negativity by allowing yourself to metamorphose. Initially you may allow that sponge to transform into a rubber ball so that all that comes your way may bounce off, but this is but a short-term measure. Instead of allowing that sponge to absorb the waters of emotion, visualise it absorbing the light of love. Allow light to fill the holes in your sponge. Light has a powerful bleaching effect and transforms the sludge of emotional waters into light, without affecting the structure of the sponge. Surround yourself with love; allow it to emanate from the core of your being encompassing it with forgiveness and compassion. Love is the greatest tool you have to assist you in your detachment from others but to be truly effective love without conditions has no hooks in it.

Having **compassion** also means kindness, concern, consideration, empathy and sympathy. As explained, being too sympathetic may cloud your function as a healer and being too compassionate may not be what the client may require. Some people would love a shoulder to cry on when in fact what they may really need is a sharp word to pull them from wallowing in self-pity. That also means being kind and later they will come to appreciate your concern.

Love also comes in many guises but in the context of healing, it relates to caring and sharing. It is not because you idolise someone or have deep affection, but you care for them at a much deeper level to the point of wholeness. You desire to see them well – for themselves. The love you need to express is more at a universal level without any conditions of ifs and buts. You just love them as a fellow interconnected being to the point of loving the soul that they are.

That feeling of total unconditional love is not often accommodated within the physical emotional program of the human mind. Few do on occasions experience the overshadowing of the essence of that condition. It may be experienced as your compassion rises with your empathy to a situation. It may also come to those who are touched by the essence of spirit, as that essence flows with the clarity of the channel. That is when you may experience the rise of the essence of unconditional love as you allow it to be, by cleansing your systems of the attachments and desires of your physicality.

It is your agenda to become that connection while in your physicality to anchor that love energy to earth. Do not allow your emotions the satisfaction to generate in a negative way but feed your love to these other dimensions of being. Your awareness at each moment, your attention in the now will assist you in allowing the essence of love to flow through you, through appreciation and gratitude and adoration to the beauty before you. Be that pure essence. It will happen if that is your will, the will of your essence and of the God within.

There is always the temptation when healing that *you want* the person to become well. Irrespective of whether it is for them, this is where your own **ego** is seeking some degree of satisfaction or self-aggrandisement. We all have an ego; it is part of who we are but where healing is concerned, keep it out of the way and allow the higher forces to do the necessary work. By allowing the energies to flow in as natural a way as possible without the influence of your own **will**, (especially for gratification of the ego) will produce the required outcome in the given circumstances. Always remember that you are an **instrument** and channel for this energy and that you **accept** and trust that what will be will be.

Reference is often made to the 'Divine Will'. Divine will comes about through your own openness to that perspective. It is the resultant conclusion due to complete openness of mind and hearts. For true healing to occur at a spiritual level there should be this openness, together with a recognition and acceptance of the condition that has been exacerbated by imbalance and harmony. Once this condition of the ego mind is achieved, there is complete openness to the higher consciousness then that space of openness may be filled with love unconditional and thus balance and healing is restored. That openness will thus bring about the appropriate reaction from the individuated Christ consciousness - that fragmented expression of the divine will.

As the healer also becomes a channel for his own divinity and is a catalyst for change in the recipient, then the healer too is an expression of the divine will.

The present modality is that the healer is encouraged to tune in or attune to that which is outside or separate from self and should be the way to avoid difficulties with the desires of the ego mind. In time, the attunement will be different as one attunes or becomes their higher nature and a direct expression of the healing essence. Healing will be effected by the divine will of the individuated Christ consciousness but always remembering that the divine will is still an expression of the universal will of the consciousness of God.

SEEDS OF HOPE

Envelop us dear Father
With the seeds of all the knowing,
Water them with your tears
Of compassion, to keep them growing.

Nourish them with your love
Through the sunshine of your might,
Raise them with your tender care
Towards the loving light.

Assist the flowers to open
In the experience of their prime,
Rejoice with them their splendour
In your glory so sublime.

Let their loving forms create
A rich harvest of so much toil,
And pass on to new beginnings
Their seeds in fertile soil.

Many healers feel that that silence and *tranquil* surroundings enhances the power of healing as indeed it may do so. As well as promoting a relaxed atmosphere for the patient, it enables the healer to attune to the source of the energy. That ambience combined with the calm of the healer may go a long way to achieving the desired outcome.

Being *human* is an essential attribute for healers. As therapists, there is often a tendency to be too professional with a demise of humour. Some clients may need cheering up and besides promoting a *positive* outlook, healers and all therapists should always maintain a sense of humour. On one occasion, a lady came for healing for a particular problem, but while we were having preliminary discussions I noticed she kept stifling a belch but I made no comment. We laid her out on the couch and just as Marion and I commenced healing, she did it again. I gently suggested, "You should do something about this wind" and without any warning I (sympathetically) broke wind.

Marion and I desperately tried to avoid eye contact until the body beneath our hands started to tremble and that did it, we all three were immersed in the hilarity of the occasion for twenty minutes. Every time we attempted to get on with the job of healing, the laughing started again, until I finally decided to stop for the session. Our client went away with the parting words, "Thank you, that was the best healing I could have received".

A healer's first *responsibility* is to him/herself. Keeping your own body in order with regular exercise, correct breathing and sustenance maintains that balance. There are so many wonderful souls around advocating their own regime, perhaps because they may have some wealth issues to address, but the key here is moderation in all things. If it suits you and does not put you under duress then that is fine. It does not mean that if you are not well you cannot heal. If you have learnt to attune to the source then that energy will flow the way it should and you may derive some benefit at the same time. There have been a number of occasions when I have felt under par for various reasons and have been asked to channel healing and the outcomes have been both positive for the client and myself. Of course, if you are feeling ill then it may well be irresponsible to continue to try to channel, you may well find that you are the recipient!

CHAPTER 10

The Dilemma With Healing

Be still and know,
all your many problems that surround you by the score,
are only meant to help you and grow a little more.
By reason and understanding and hearing what is said,
will only allow your love to glow and keep you in good stead.

The application of healing is not a problem but there are other concepts to be aware of and to overcome. Over the centuries, healing has been an integral part of religious doctrine especially in the Christian tradition, which the church has tended to monopolise. More pertinently because of the reputation of its founder who many hold in such high esteem and awe, there has been reluctance by many to attempt to heal. He is reputed to have said 'greater things will you do' and only now, two thousand years later latent healers are coming into their own power. Perhaps the rise in the use of healing as a therapy may be as the result of an interest in Reiki and therapeutic touch, which have no religious connotations and uses the universal energy to heal.

By far the largest hurdle that any aspirant would have to overcome is **confidence.** Healing is such an airy-fairy subject with so many variables that it is very much like stepping into the unknown and the simplest way of finding out if the healing has worked is to ask the client/patient. The key then is to be patient until you have tried it a few times and you can **relax** more into what you are doing and trying to achieve.

Clients also have to be patient. There is an inclination with some people to expect a miracle when they receive healing, based on their misconceptions about faith and belief issues. Since they regard themselves short on faith, they are likely not to bother to try healing. Healing may take **time**, perhaps over a period of weeks or even months to produce the desired effect so **patience** on the part of healer and client is not only desirable but also important.

I always insist at our healing workshops that both 'healer' and 'patient' give feedback to the group to share and acknowledge their

83

individual experience and to understand that there are so many variables within the group. Even now after all these years of sharing healing I ask clients to share their experience, not to boost my confidence, although I am still not always aware of any interchange of energy, but to acknowledge that they have received or feel something a little bit different. Because also of my inquisitive nature I do desire to know what, energetically, is going on within their body.

The actual benefit any one person receives may depend on a number of factors.

In the first instance there needs to be a rapport between the healer and the patient and the responsibility for this rests squarely on the shoulders of the healer. Their general attitude, courteousness and consideration for the patient do go a long way to build up that confidence and an explanation by the healer of their method of working. It is so important for the patient to relax as much as possible before the healing experience. This opens them up more to the healing energies and *relaxation* alone permits a boost to the immune system.

Similarly, healers need to get themselves 'psyched' up or *attuned* to the source of their energy, to relax and open up, allowing any personal emotions or desires to dissolve away and becoming a clear a channel as possible for the healing energy. The simplest way to do this is to *ask* or *intend* that you be used in this way. In the appendices, I have included an introductory healing sequence for guidance purposes.

Earlier I mentioned about the need to keep the ego out of the way whilst healing for the reasons mentioned but it is important here to mention the power of *intention.* For general healing, it is your intention to be a conduit for the healing energy and for those that are students and healers who just wish 'to be' that is all the intention that is required.

Environmental factors may also have a bearing on the efficacy of healing. It may for instance be necessary to give comfort and healing in a pedestrianised area with the attendant noises, inquisitive natures and odd looks. If the healer has learned to manage his *detachment* and if he feels it appropriate considering the needs of his client and the client is happy in the circumstances then it is all right to do so. A number of times I have been in the right place at the right time; in a shop, in a busy high street, a restaurant or in an office if I felt it right to offer healing then it occurred and very often, it was a successful outcome.

It can also be very difficult approaching a complete stranger to offer healing, but it is possible using a little psychology. By at first offering a little sympathy (it is quite useful at times like these), asking what treatment they have had and whether they have tried healing will determine their readiness to accept any. Similarly, a gentle prolonged touch or a hand on the shoulder if you are a naturally tactile person will produce the right effect.

No matter how much they desire a healing, some people put up their own barriers to healing by using the illness as a **crutch** and not doing enough to promote their own health. The crutch may be the sympathy they desire to support their own illness but this eventually wears a bit thin after time has elapsed and especially if they live their illness twenty-four hours a day. To illustrate this scenario, two women who were friends in common both with M.E. came for healing. One subsequently took up tai chi and other inspiring activities and made remarkable progress overcoming her illness whilst the other lived and breathed M.E. eventually confining herself to a motorised wheelchair.

Using illness as a crutch to bring about a change in lifestyle is more common than one would imagine, the main emphasis being to give up work and do something more creative or recreational. I longed to leave work once my healing ability had taken off but I realise now we would not have been where we are now with a pension to exist and be happy as well. We met an incapacitated bank manager in Scotland who was sick from work with a 'severe' neck problem. He passed his time at home renovating his fishing boat! A few other individuals at work also had their 'problems' and did very little to encourage improvement until they had secured invalidity pension. I am not suggesting that they were not suffering but merely making a statement about using illness as a crutch. Others may suffer illness or pain perhaps because of a lesson they need to understand or experience.

As a healer you have to learn to be **non-judgemental** with respect to the personality, how deserving they are or whether healing would actually help them. We are all making judgements from day to day about different issues even though we qualify them with discernment and constructive criticism, which are at the healthy end of the spectrum. If we can relate each sentient being as a spark of divinity, then since we are all sparks of the whole, who are we to stand in judgement of another part of the whole?

The degree of another's spirituality or the space in which they occupy is often a matter of criticism and judgement by another. All are on a pathway of their own spiritual evolution, indeed to fulfill their own spiritual destiny and all will complete that journey because that is their desire, from the deepest level of their being. All are at different points along that journey, some at cross-roads, others are up blind alleys, some even move backwards but each always return to tread their spiritual pathway.

When they have seen the light, many appear to journey quickly but in their deep desire for self, they forget that they are all part of each other, part of the creative oneness of all. From the grander perspective of where they are, they look down on their brothers and sisters at their closed hearts and minds and criticise because they do not see the light and love around them. How can they see and feel that light and love as the shadow of your judgement bars their way? Step aside, hold out your hand, love unconditionally their situation because you too have been there and gently encourage their progress.

It should be understood that every being is meant to be exactly where they are on their own journey, through the choices they have made and by desires of the ego or guidance from their higher perspective. If they choose not to move forward then there may be good karmic reasons. It is not for another to judge and to know the lessons that being has come to learn. It is not for you also to judge another for their lack of interest or scepticism in your spiritual pursuits. They may not need the experience of your journey because they may have already travelled that road in another existence. They may even be waiting for you to catch them up and your judgments will provide you with a burden to make your pace slower. Let them observe your progress and the unconditional love you are able to radiate and when the time is right they too will be able to fuse with that love if they so wish.

Some also judge others because of their apparent ignorance of spiritual matters. Not all the knowledge that has been gathered in a lifetime makes you a spiritual master - only an author of another book. Wisdom comes with the recognition of the lessons of experience and the practice of the teachings and if you were an adept of spiritual disciplines, you would not judge another. Others may be apparently ignorant because that is their way, which is where they are at this time. It is for you to see and learn from the other qualities that they have mastered like just being in that space.

Judgement is a shadow in the form of a mirror. It reflects back to you what you need to know about yourself, perhaps pride, jealousy or unconditional love that you may need to develop. So try not to judge another harshly, but critical observation can be constructive if expressed with unconditional love. You are all on the pathway to fulfill your destiny, to become at one with the creative essence of all. For as you judge that essence in another you also judge yourself, for you are the same. As you walk your pathway, your essence becomes brighter and there is no greater service one can perform for another than to hold out a hand to them, stand aside and allow your light to shine forth on their pathway.

There have been occasions where I had thought that maybe a person would not accept or consider healing as an option, purely based on my opinion of the person I saw and consequently I did not therefore suggest healing. Then Marion would take the initiative and before long, that person would grasp the opportunity resulting in a successful healing outcome. I received a reminder once again, that having fixed opinions brings home some important teachings.

We forget sometimes why we become ill. Illness and disease is the result from our cumulative reactions and emotions to situations, which we repress or store in our bodies. The illness says 'stop' repressing these emotions, which causes an imbalance subsequently reflected through pain. The body is saying 'I hurt' and is really asking us to stop and reflect on its causes and a change in thought behaviour can often bring about a release. Therefore, we have to **surrender** by letting go of fears and any form of negativity that may ultimately be a contribution towards our illnesses and diseases.

Sometimes people are very reluctant to open up in a very direct way, it is up to the healer then to become more aware to secure more information about the condition and relevant information will surface in some way.

Listen to the words and to the feelings expressed at a deeper level. Listen to the meaning behind the words as you would listen to your own thoughts of guidance if you would take that time to be still. As you would

87

listen to your own still small voice or telepathic communications with your higher consciousness or that of the beings around you, then use that same space to listen to what another's higher guidance is telling you to lead you into ways in which you are able to assist them. Others need a catalyst - one who has secured an attunement to the higher vibrations and through this, much release of emotional baggage.

Indeed keys will be given to unlock the doors that bar their own pathway and only then will they be able to pass through when they are ready to remove the burdens they carry. Their pathway is in a sense an uphill climb and it will only become easier by removal of their own burdens, for the burdens they carry are their physical attachments, emotions and mental attitudes that tie them to physicality.

We try with many of our clients to reflect on the pain, illness or disease to ascertain the possible contributory factors resulting through negative thought patterns or repressed emotions and as a guide go back at least two years before the manifestation of the problem. Invariably they come up with some traumatic event or situation that they have not let go. The key as to whether the matter has been dealt with, is in their present emotional reaction when they bring the matter up. Of course the root causes of illnesses are not limited to just two years some go back to childhood, pre-natal existence or even a past life experience. Children are so good at shutting away their fears, pretending they do not exist until something triggers them to the surface in later years. Whilst in the womb the child can feel the emotions of the mother, perhaps even to understand the thoughts at a deeper level and acts how it feels appropriate as it matures.

The effect of past lives can be such a daunting experience, but so many now accept the principle that we have all lived before. The law of **karma** or cause and effect can play an integral part in our journey, in helping us to understand our spirituality. It tries to teach us that we just cannot go around poking people's eyes out, it is not very spiritual. So in order for us to learn that lesson we just might develop that affliction to bring home the understanding. Many times I have heard the clichéd expression 'It must be my karma …' the acceptance of it is not enough, it is far more important to wrap that acceptance with the gift of compassion and the ribbons of understanding.

ANOTHER TIME

If we had met a thousand years ago
It would not have been the same,
We may have been two different people
Playing a different game.
Perhaps we were only touching
Giving us something to face,
Expanding the feelings in future
In another time and place.
This may even be happening now
Taking it forward to distant time,
Emotions to express themselves
Into a future life sublime.
It matters not what we were
What we are or where we've been
But the sum of all our experiences
In all the world's we've seen.

A friend was troubled for many years with pains in the thigh and confined to a wheelchair for a great deal of time. He tried past life therapy and was regressed to the Napoleonic wars when he was mortally wounded resulting from an injury to the thigh. The trauma seemed apparently to be carried forward into the present life, perhaps there were other implications. It does help sometimes in recognising and accepting that a reason helps in coming to terms with the pain or illness. This friend subsequently visited Knocke, a place of pilgrimage in Ireland and now spends more time out of the wheelchair!

Although healing works in mysterious ways and can work through an energy exchange via the human energy field without the need for dialogue but *counselling* is important. Giving time for the client for permission to unlock those fears and traumas and *helping* them though suggestions of *positive* thoughts and actions are part of the healing process. *Positive intention* can only bring positive results.

In the early days of my attempts to heal I just wanted to share it somewhat indiscriminately, I could see so many in need and I could give them an option of a way out of their difficulty, so my enthusiasm landed me in a few embarrassing situations. I held back after being ridiculed a few times and learnt to use a little psychology of approach. Other issues already mentioned in that the person may not yet be ready for healing. For these reasons, you must always wait for that person to *ask* for it.

A point of contention amongst many healers is whether to charge for their services. Many do regard it as a gift and give it freely not expecting any recompense. I tried charging a fee at one time, it lasted a week! We felt very uncomfortable and since then we have relied on donations. A lot depends on the circumstances of the healer, whether they are setting up a practice and are dependant on the income to cover overheads. It is as well to remember that a labourer is worthy of his hire and priests, doctors and other therapists charge for their services.

The energy of money is used to manipulate those minds and bodies that are without or are lacking. It is a gift indeed to be able to increase the energy of a substance with very little work involved, but consider the motive behind the desire. If used for the benefit of all without self-deprivation, then that energy is used for the good. It is good to learn the pain of sacrifice only if you can let the pain go. If used for self-aggrandisement, to command the respect of another, to make another less equal, then that energy has been abused.

There is much to commend the system of bartering - giving in exchange some thing that one needs and arriving at a level for what is acceptable to both sides. A rich man can afford to give more and a poor man gives less but the giver is happy because he gives according to need and receives appropriately. It is true that your physical bodies need sustenance to clothe the body, to provide shelter, and to honour responsibilities. For this money is required because your society demands that that should be the way.

There are those, however, who by use and abuse of the gifts that they have, find it easy to receive more than their labour is worth in spite of the enlightenment and awareness they bring. There may be karmic implications in that situation but for the teachers who have abused their responsibilities of sharing their gifts, there may be greater ones.

The gifts of the spirit are indeed free for all and a teacher is worthy to receive energies for the energy they share. It is like a harvest of the seeds you sow and nourish.

Energy should be exchanged, though not necessarily money, but be assured that when an energy is given with love, untainted by greed, desire, power, then that love will be returned with gratitude in abundance. It is in trusting and knowing from within, that all will be well, when all is balanced in the scales of the universe. Each shall receive fair exchange for the worth they have given and equivalent exchange when given at the expense of another.

Although we are ostensibly working full time as healers running a healing centre, the donations we receive adequately equate to what a therapist may receive for their time and effort. There are of course exceptions, like the woman who came with various allergies and physical problems for five sessions. She parted with a great deal of money when visiting doctors overseas and what did she donation did she leave? Zero. Healing incidentally did a lot more for her than all the other orthodox and complementary treatments she tried. At the other end of the spectrum a man, suffering from terminal cancer donated a lot more than he subscribed to a famous and reputable healer because he felt that he had derived a far greater benefit. He moved on eventually but the quality of his life was much improved.

Healing is like a bank account:

> *the more deposits you make of love and compassion*
> *the more interest you earn in peace and harmony.*

General Summary

Summarising the salient points in the last two chapters we can remember with the acronym:

Detachment
Ego
Acceptance, **A**sk
Love

Will
Instrument
Tranquillity, **T**ime
Humanity

Compassion, **C**onfidence, **C**rutch, **C**ounselling
Relaxation
Attunement
Positive, **P**atience

That is what healers do in essence; deal with other people's crap. As long as you do not compost it in your own backyard, your healing flowers will grow abundantly.

CHAPTER 11

Happenings

Be still and know,
your loved ones are a thought away from the message of your heart –
a bond of common language while you are apart.
Attract them not for pity's sake to bring them very near,
they can only come no closer than the barrier of your fear.
So after they are parted and you have set them free,
share with them my happiness in bringing them to me.

What happens when healing takes place? As previously mentioned science knows very little about the mechanics of healing but is only aware of the theoretical principles involved. The way science is progressing, it will only be a matter of time before there is substantiation that there is a transfer of energy between healer and client. It has however been proved that a change in the brain wave patterns occur when one relaxes and even though induced by the healer is not proven. Therefore, for the present time we have to rely on anecdotal evidence from both healer and client.

The Experience of the Healer

My own experience of the energy effects of healing have been minimal over the years, which have been rather frustrating at times although now I accept that is the way it is meant for me to better understand the subject.

After attunement, the healer may experience waves of energy coming down though the head or up from the solar plexus and down the arms into the hands, which may be in the form of tingling sensations or maybe nothing at all. In my experience, facilitating workshops all over the U.K. men seem less likely to be objectively aware of energy movements within the body. Perhaps we may be just thick or to put it a little more delicately a little less sensitive than women. The norm is for most healers to feel heat in the hands or fingers, the central core of the energy seeming to emanate from the palm of the hand.

Occasionally the healer may feel some discomfort or even pain. This may give an indication of where healing is required and the healer should act accordingly. Empathy on behalf of the healer could be at work in these circumstances as also it could be guidance from a deeper intuitive level to direct the healer where to place the hands. There have been suggestions that the healer is absorbing the clients "stuff". Perhaps this may be so but if a healer is working the way he should there is no need to take on other people's garbage.

As the healer develops, he may receive intuitive guidance as to where to locate the hands, which may not necessarily be at the site of the problem. The guidance may be in the form of mental direction or simply the ability to home in to a problem. Sometimes by "scanning" the body with one or both hands hot or cold spots may be detected which would indicate some attention is required in that area. This would not necessarily mean that there is a physiological problem but maybe an imbalance in the energy system. There is a danger here of putting the client in a state of alarm or distress especially when the healer suggests there is something wrong. It is far better to suggest that there may be an energy imbalance and for the client to get it checked by the G.P. if a problem manifests in that area.

Intuitive guidance is a wonderful tool to assist in the healing process but not as a diagnostic tool. A qualified medical practitioner, who is clinically responsible for the patient, should be the only person to make a diagnosis. This is included in the code of conduct adopted by reputable healing organisations. There are however exceptionally gifted healers who are able to diagnose with remarkable accuracy through their intuitive guidance. They are able to see subjectively, exactly what is happening in that area of the part of the body under duress.

The Experience of the Client

Clients also may experience different energies in the form of heat, cold, tingling sensations, a numbness or a 'lightness'. Everyone's reaction is different depending on his or her particular problem and his or her energy interaction with the healer. No one ever comes to any harm because of healing but there may be occasions where some discomfort of even heightened pain may be experienced. It is as though the pain is taking its last breath before its demise. A number of clients I have worked with endured deep heat and a burning sensation and one woman convinced that she had been scorched went to check in the mirror! Whatever she had, had been probably cauterised – spiritually speaking.

To illustrate another effect of pain whilst healing we had a call from our friend Cynthia one day, who had broken her ankle whilst on holiday in Portugal. The hospital doctors set it wrapped it in plaster and sent her home. She hinted that it was still very painful so we went to do the business. She felt a great deal of heat through the plaster, some movement of the bones as though they were being manipulated and even more pain. I felt intuitively that it had not been set properly, (although it would not take a psychic to guess that) so she went to the hospital for an x-ray and put right the dilemma. She was also informed that she would never walk properly again but with regular healing over the next few months, some intuitive physiotherapy, dogged determination on her part the foot returned to normality.

Nearly all who receive healing report the feeling of being relaxed or being on a cloud and some resent returning to normality as if after a deep sleep. It is surprising also, that even those who have great difficulty in relaxing, slip into the soporific effect of the healing energy. Two particular clients were able, after lying or sitting down with the intention of me to commence healing were away with the fairies before I had even started.

Some people whilst receiving healing are aware of perceiving colours. This to me gives some indication of the healing energy given at that time. I suggest that they use that colour in their own visualisations for self- healing until they no longer feel it necessary. Whilst on the subject of colour there are colour therapists around who probably excel at what they do and make assumptions about what colours people need based on their acquired knowledge. Personally, I do not agree that colours are suggested for the patient in this way unless the therapist can intuitively sense what colour or colours the patient needs.

Aura healing is popular with some healers in that they work in the client's energy field or aura, without physically touching the body. This process should be explained, (as with any form of healing) in that the recipient may be a little slower experiencing the effect of the energy than by direct touch. Direct touch usually has the effect of being immediately comforting and healing.

Effects of Healing

Instantaneous happenings or miracles are not the norm when we talk about the effects of healing although they do occur. We have been fortunate on some occasions, to witness a dramatic change in a condition and complete relief of pain. All it means is that all the conditions are right for the healing to take place, especially with respect to the emotional and mental attitude of the client.

Usually there is some sort of improvement to the condition, if not the physical relief of pain then mentally or emotionally, they are more able to cope with the condition. Sometimes the discomfort or pain may be as much as eighty percent improved and may continue to improve over the next few hours or days, or it may be necessary to have follow-up sessions over a few weeks or months to effect an amelioration of the condition.

If after several sessions, nothing happens and another healer has been 'tried' or other appropriate therapies, then it is worth considering that perhaps there are other issues that may be needed to be addressed by the client to bring about the required changes.

One change that we are unable to prevent is the transition of death. We can be certain that at some stage in our earthly existence our spirit will leave this earth, the shell of the body just goes into decay. We have received requests a number of times to visit a terminally ill relative to give healing. We know what they are hoping for and we are aware that the time has arrived for a parting. We share that special energy, comfort them and through the healing, help them to relax so that they may pass on with peace and dignity.

Often when there is a lingering illness with no hopeful prognosis, it is useful to try to engage them in positive conversation about their future expectations in relation to a continued existence. A large proportion of humanity has a faith or belief system, which includes some scenario of a hereafter and as one approaches the ultimate scenario of this life, more time is set aside to thinking about the possibilities and outcomes. If it is possible, we should lead them into dialogue and try to help allay any fears they may have. Fears do surface if they have time to think about what will happen when they pass over. Fears also surface with the relatives; of what it would be like if their loved one moved on and what will become of them. The relatives also need comfort and healing and to be given the strength to encourage the loved one to let go. So many hold on to the sick person for their own sakes when in fact we should all be able to recognise when the time has come to say our goodbyes we should celebrate their life and wish them well on their future journey.

At this point, mention should be made of the placebo effect. A placebo is a panacea, a cure-all, magic potion or just an excuse. It is also the by-product of a suggestion or an expectation sometimes linked with faith on the part of the recipient. Experiments have been scientifically conducted to test the efficacy of healing against placebo healing where non-healers go through the physical motions without apparently channelling the healing energy. The results were inconclusive because some of the placebo healers were also having some positive results. So why was this occurring?

As mentioned earlier some healers have a natural tendency to heal without being conscious of their intentions and the placebo healers were doing nothing more than what comes naturally. Just by doing creates some sort of intention and if that placebo healer has a positive attitude and abundant vitality, the placebo healing also works. Similarly, with the expectations of the client their own intention can create self-healing along with the placebo support administered.

In essence placebo or not, does it really matter how one gets well so long as there are some positive benefits?

Summary of the Effects of Healing

It is all in the **MIND**:

> **M**iracles do happen when the time is right
> **I**mprovement is the norm
> **N**othing may happen if the time is not right
> **D**eath will happen when the time is right

97

THE PROMISE

When one travels from your world
In permanence and alone,
Be sure that I will meet them
And take them to their home.

I will find them there a place of rest
To sleep and gain strength anew,
Then they will see horizons
That only they can view.

All the love that they have given
Is stored within a chest,
Which will then be opened
When they have had their rest.

This chest of jewels will open
And radiate such wealth,
Of happiness and pure pleasure
Which will restore their health.

Do not grieve in sadness
Nor for your pity's sake,
Send them onward with your love
For you will follow in their wake.

They may come and visit you
To cheer your lonely day,
So be sure you are not crying
It may well bar their way.

Be glad that they have found a place
That they can call again,
A place of solace like their home
Where they are free from pain.

Many mansions will they visit
To suit the seasons of their soul,
But they will do their choosing
To reach the greatest goal.

Know your loved one will come yet closer
For we shall never part,
Their love will only magnify
In the bosom of my heart.

CHAPTER 12

Intention

Be still and know,
my mind is totally open to what you are intending,
combining that with what I am so that we can create a mending.

From the beginning, most of my time spent healing was by following my intuition to some degree, putting my hands where I felt was necessary and of course, where the client wanted the direct help or intervention. I did not follow any set procedures. In the main people felt a great deal of heat, which I regarded as would be a normal reaction from most healers. Occasionally clients reported that a movement of pain had occurred or something was going on inside the body in the form of a localised cooling, movements, tingling or 'electrical' sensations.

I did not pay too much attention to the detail and just accepted it as straightforward spiritual healing together with receiving some extra help from our discarnate friends.

The way I tended to give healing, was to work initially on the head to primarily relax the client and go directly to the area requiring attention. As the healing developed and Marion and I worked together, she tended to work on balancing the energies and I continued to home in on the problem.

Over the years, clients have presented us with numerous problems and conditions and many have felt improvements some with instantaneous benefits. During the healing sequence I did not particularly tune in to any source or the patient, because I felt that it was 'on tap' whenever it was required. I took it for granted. When I worked, I sometimes went into a bit of a daydream state and when I gave talks, I managed to demonstrate healing and answer questions at the same time. It seemed to work satisfactorily.

When I facilitated workshops however, I delivered it in such a way that would be healers should focus in on their source of healing to whom or whatever that was, according to their belief system or religious persuasion. This prevented an ego problem developing and by placing the responsibility for healing elsewhere. This just allowed healing to take place without the interference of personal desires for success, thus enabling the healing energy to produce the best outcome.

It was not until I was into facilitating my first two-year healing course that I began to feel that I could do far more effective healing or I was being inspired to think that way. I had developed certain techniques over the years in the way I held my hands and used my fingers whilst healing. It was different from just holding the hands on or near the site of the problem; I felt I was being more involved in the healing process.

Therefore, when I needed a shove one comes along. On another issue, I visited a medium quite unknown to me and she told me I would be doing psychic surgery and would be able to see what was going on internally. That would be interesting I thought. So I waited but not for long. I made discreet enquiries from two other mediums that 'crossed' my pathway and the message was the same.

Now psychic surgery to me was literally opening up the body and going inside as psychic surgeons do in the Philippines or South America but in the first world countries there is less likely to this happening perhaps out of spiritual respect to our medical profession. Many healers do have their helpers, perhaps doctors and nurses who wish to continue with their work. I would prefer to call this cohesive healing as **spirit surgery** or **spirit intervention.**

I started feeling and getting myself more involved in the activity of healing. I had a scant knowledge but not fully conversant with anatomy and physiology but I began to use my imagination and powers of visualisation far more.

I visualised a laser beam from my fingers to burn out and destroy diseased tissue, a syringe to inject lubricating fluid into joints and sometimes a gentle massage or stroking motion to remove pain, invariably improvising and using various visualisation techniques to assist in ameliorating the condition. In the healing fraternity this stroking effect may be considered or interpreted as inappropriate touching, so healers should be cognisant of such actions. I have found sometimes that by lightly stroking down the arms or legs the client felt the movement of pain down the limb and drawn out of the fingers or toes. It is recorded, that Valentine Greatrakes, a healer of the seventeenth century used a similar technique with reportedly great success.

I was finding healing was more beneficial particularly where people were having either chronic or acute pain. Often we had requests to deal with a spate of back problems, arthritic conditions, nerve problems or fractures. Healing may also help in pre or post-operative procedures. As some women will know, the after effects of radiotherapy following mastectomy can be extremely sore and restrict arm movements, but we have worked with a few that have felt instant and continued relief after one session. Another had suffered for twelve years after an epidural injection and again felt considerable relief after one session of healing.

Some pains experienced in the body may be referred pain emanating from the spinal column and by working on the appropriate area of the spine relief may be experienced. I found in some circumstances I tended to place my fingers without pressure either side of the area and allow the team do their stuff. Pain manifesting as blockages, may also be released by using fingertips on the energy meridians and acupuncture points. My knowledge in this area was next to negligible but I felt I was working more on an intuitive level.

From my accumulated experiences, I began to realise that healers could be more effective by including a basic anatomy and knowledge of energy meridians and acupuncture points. I had impressed students of healing to keep their selves out of the way during the process and I felt that this was the correct method at least to start with.

Through my progression as a healer, I began naturally to focus my attention on the problem presented to me for a positive outcome and I began to question whether it was up to me to contribute to the requirements of the client. Then I asked 'Why do we have doctors?' They apply their skills to specific problems, so why cannot healers have more input into what they are doing?

We know the healing energy will flow to wherever it is required but a concentration or focus of energy on specific areas with the intention of a desired outcome and with attunement to the inter-dimensional helpers, would have a more beneficial effect.

This is where the **power of intention** comes into its own. If the healer uses their intentions to overcome the problem through their compassion for the subject and not for personal gratification then why not introduce that input. The best way to assist in this process is using the mind in visualising change, imagining whatever tools are required to produce an effective outcome.

Often regarded as a personal endeavour or even a promise to oneself, intentions often lack the tenacity, perseverance or drive to achieve or attain the objective.

The essential aspect of any intention is to combine it with the universal energy and to provide it in service and to ensure it is for the higher good of those involved. It is good to use the power of intention to work with the universal energies, leaving the personal will aside, allowing and having no attachment to the outcome. This broader use of intention is best used when healing.

Intention can be also be used to greater effect especially when working directly with the agencies of spirit. This requires a focus on the direction and outcome but still with a detachment, especially when related to personal desires. It is the focus of intent with access to all 'equipment' available, that will produce the desired effect. It is being open and allowing these specifics to operate that will produce the desired results.

For some time now, I have had an intuitive feeling that healing modalities will change over the coming decades and healers will need to be open to those possibilities. We are experiencing investigations into stem cell and genetic research in the physical reality so why should not our spiritual counterparts be also able to experiment with the same parts energetically. The study of quantum physics tells us that all matter is energy vibrating at different rates and that the physical reality is an illusion, it is not solid at all. So energies are able to interact on each other and work together effectively when co-joined by the power of intention thus having a common cause.

It is also generally accepted amongst healers that the healing energy emanates from the palms of the hands, this being the position of an energy centre or chakra but we also have the ability to channel or direct that energy, however we feel is appropriate, using fingers, our heart or our big toe! The important tool we are using is our mind - the conductor of the orchestra.

Focussing the mind with intention can be a strain and a drain for some healers but it is not always necessary to hold that intention for the duration of the healing. Leaving yourself open for inspiration will allow you to visualise what is required at the appropriate time, although the time element does not come into the healing equation. The intention is a directed energy input placed in the matrix of the universal consciousness and will be absorbed from the matrix when it is appropriate.

When I learned of the concept of 'having' a healing centre, the idea seemed altruistic but really did not know what it meant or what the implications would be. We just nursed the idea and by visiting other healing and holistic centres, we began to formulate opinions and ideas and thus developed our intention. We held that focus until we arrived at Peacehaven. Then we developed many other intentions.

We intended that we would demolish the existing barns and erect a new building, using as a healing and spiritual teaching centre. We held that focussed intention for the future because to create such an enterprise requires finance. I spent a lot of time creating business plans and applying for grants to assist in the process but to no avail. In our hearts, we were not designing our efforts for a business so we felt uncomfortable with that process. Whilst finances were required, I also focussed on what we lacked in that direction which brought me great discomfort.

I began to examine why these intentions were not materialising. I had not harnessed the power of intention in the correct way. By also concentrating on our apparent lack and since like attracts like, our goalposts were moved, not further away but sideways in an effort for us to refocus.

The other resolution that radiated from the processes was discomfort. What made the discomfort? Was there a feeling that something was not right? Now when it comes to treading where angels fear to then I will face the challenge without foolhardiness because without extending our boundaries and opening our box, we can never make progress and by not experiencing the dark can we experience the light. The discomfort was more to do with something not being right. I was out of alignment or balance with who I was and my purpose. I was out of alignment with the non-physical part of me and my ego mind was assuming control. What I realised is that when you really feel enthusiastic, passionate, stimulated about a creative process you become aligned to your source and expressing that essence. You feel more balanced.

You are here to experiment as a creator in the physical existence, to learn how to create, using the essence that is within you. You have free will to do this and you have as much guidance as you desire, it is all down to your choice in the matter.

Just as you have your mentors in the physical reality such as your parents, teachers and even children, there are those in other realities that are willing to share, teach and facilitate your passage through a life but allowing you to make your choices. Closer to home there is your own guidance system which may be termed as your soul, source or higher self. This other aspect of yourself is who you really are and you as an individual are only a small part of the whole, here to expand and take your life experience back to the whole. Your soul is always accessible to you, if you desire it is always there supporting you for your greatest advantage and well-being.

Your soul does not want you to suffer and does not want you to make your life difficult. It or god does not bring suffering on you for you to learn a lesson about life. It is what you attract by your wanting. This is one of the greatest gifts you have brought with you into this reality - the power to create through wanting and the tool you have developed to help you in this process is your mind.

*There is a convention in the universe, which states that **like attracts like**. There are no exceptions, whatever you focus upon you attract - the good, the bad and the ugly. So whatever you bring into your life you have wanted it at some level, you have desired it, you have attracted it to you, through the power of creation that is part of you. Whatever you have created has responded to the power of your thoughts, whatever you have given attention to and the amount of **attention** or focussing you have given **will manifest** that object or circumstance **eventually**.*

The power of attraction has two edges, it does not differentiate between good and bad, right or wrong that is the purpose of the individual in making their own choice. Attraction happens in such a way that it depends on the state of mind of the individual. If they are happy, joyful, positive, loving then they will attract only those vibrations to them. If they are unhappy, negative and hurting then those vibrations will only continue and magnify. Whatever is wanted will happen. There are no exceptions. It is only time that could be considered as your greatest ally because it gives you space to change the scenario which you have asked for.

In wanting and focussing on something positive in your life it will be attracted to you, depending on intention and clarity of focus but if you include 'ifs' or 'buts' in the equation you push the focus of your attention further away. Your own thinking process has asked for two things at once and the object of your desire has not materialised. As your focus centres more on what you do not want, or your lack of something then you are attracting more of the same. That is the law. It is the act of focussing and **what you focus on brings forth the creation.**

As an example, you may focus your thoughts in such a way that you want a big house but you may also say that you have not got the money or you cannot afford it. What you have done is that you have negated your request or pushed it out of reach and if you focus more on the lack of the necessary finances, you will never have your big house.

Whenever you need help in making a decision or attracting something into your life, just ask and listen to your thoughts or the thoughts of your own guidance system. If you cannot hear then try examining how you feel, consider your emotional response to the issue or focus. Your emotions are your own guidance system and link you to your higher perspective, which only wants the best for you. If you are focussing on something that you do not want and you are feeling upset, angry and in discord, your higher self is providing you with a key to open the door of opportunity to make a change in the way of thinking or behaving for the better. Similarly if you are feeling inspired, or enthusiastic about something your own guidance is telling you to go for it. Happiness and joy aligns you with your higher self and you are here to share that vibration at the physical level.

The key here is to look and focus on the positive aspects of life and attract those vibrations to you. Your thoughts are magnetic and especially when you can see the object of your focus and can visualise them together with the full expectation of that creation then it will be attracted to you and become manifest.

You may be in such a state of confusion and wallowing in your own pit of despair that you cannot climb out because you have allowed yourself to be a victim. Clawing out whilst trying to be positive can be strenuous and debilitating work, so to shift some of the burden you can start by asking that you want to know what you are here to do and then be attentive to things and ideas that are presented to you and some may come to you by *obscure ways. When something really appeals to you then that is a signal from your higher self that is an opportunity to follow or that you have made the correct choices.*

You are all divine beings here in the physical life to allow yourself to express your potential and to be joyful creators in that experience. How you do that is your choice.

Intentions therefore need to be clear with positive outcomes and not focussing on the present deficiencies. The same is with regard to healing intention if you take your focus away from the existing scenario and the attached possibilities, holding on to joyful outcomes will produce positive results.

CHAPTER 13

Awareness

Be still and know,
If you cannot look at nature and hear the plaintive call,
then you will not feel the glory and the love within it all;
you will be without a knowing of the beauty at your hand,
to feel the love of nature and the fruits of this her land.

During my infant years after leaving the east end of London for the countryside of Essex, I developed an interest in nature, fostered by my primary school teacher at the time. I took long walks to my parent's vexation, investigating the natural world around me and they demonstrated more than once how annoyed they were at my prolonged absences from home, be it only for four or five hours.

My interests developed further, from regular trips to the allotment, gardening, tending, growing, geology and fossil hunting. I was interested in the mechanics of life followed later with the study of evolution of the species. In hindsight, I can see the greater picture towards my interest now in our spiritual evolution. It is almost as if there is a plan for us, a journey for us to experience and to achieve some unseen objective.

My love of nature also provided respite, shining a little light during my dark nights of the soul. A strange expression that, because our spirit never dies nor is it shrouded in the dark. It is through our egotistical experiences that we feel so deserted in times of tribulation, when we feel a sense of separation, or desertion. Only when we have reached the pit of despair do we call out for help from that benign presence that we call God.

Is it not possible that a call in the dark is also a cry for help, for to answer that call may provide a release of fear, of apprehension or of a sense of loss? Many have experienced that dark night of the soul when one feels trapped in the pit of despair.

Those that become stuck in the quagmire of their own choosing take this course of action because they know no other way. They have become lost

CALL ON ME

When you are enduring pain
and the future isn't bright,
call on me to heal you
and embrace you with my light.
When you are so lonely
and surrounded by despair,
call on me to cherish you
for I am always there.
I will enfold you with my embrace
and wipe away your tears,
prepare you for your future
and release you from your fears.
We will climb your hill together,
I will carry you in your need
to secure for you a foothold
and even take your lead.
Know I am always with you
and when your journey is done,
that in that place of stillness
another battle is won.

to their connection to a more benign reality even though that is physical. They have forgotten how good a physical life can be.

The key here is to help connect them to a moment of joy in their past experience and to build on that, like the building blocks for a house using the tools of imagination and intuition and the beauty and form of nature.

Part of your understanding in coming into the physical reality is to forget your connections but to have the free will to discover who you really are. In discovering that, you will begin to anchor the essence of your spirit into the physical reality. Those that feel totally disconnected have severed themselves from their spirituality through circumstance but help is always there, they only have to ask. Recognise also that some cannot and are unable to ask, they feel imprisoned, but that too is part of their journey.

I often refer to an analogy demonstrating the effect and power of light; when people feel enmeshed in their darkness, they liken their situation to a darkened room:

...take a light into a dark room and it will become lighter but if you could take darkness into a room of light, there will always be light....

There is always light, the sun is always shining no matter what circumstances you attract. When your body cannot sustain your spirit any longer, you are temporarily in the shadow and received into the true light of spirit. There are many such shadow experiences on your journey back to the godhead, as you are disengaged from the light, mainly through your fears and indeed it is your fears that prevent you from moving into the light, it is your state of mind that is still in the shadow.

These times of despair, are also a time of testing for the mettle of your soul. Each situation has the potential within it for a positive outcome, for the sun to shine once more. A time of shadow may come about at any time especially in times of complacency, when it is desirable that you make a shift or you need to make some progression by dealing with a situation in an appropriate way and should also be considered for reflection and introspection.

By bringing a little light, joy or love into a difficult situation can only bring an improvement or respite, which may be enough to light up the way forward.

Time and problems of life flew effortlessly by when I became locked in observation, touching, feeling, being the wild flower bending to the gentle breeze or opening up to warmth of the life giving energy of the sun. Watching the wild birds and waders showed how oblivious they are to 'when' and 'how', living only in the moment because that is all that counts. How simple nature is in its diversity and the natural scheme of things, growing, flourishing, fruiting and decaying, continually recycling.

So I became aware of the natural world around me from the innocence of a child and the blindness of adulthood, which again was my teacher because I had not yet learned to listen to my spiritual mentors. That education was a good foundation because in times of strife it has been a doorway to the greater realities and understanding of life.

Awareness means that you can attach to it all the qualities of your senses and appreciate the beauty of that which is on offer. Awareness happens when you stop thinking and enables the intelligence of your soul to come to the fore.

Your climates have an effect on your awareness. Many live a long winter through the summer months because perhaps the weather has not been psychologically to their liking. However, your awareness changes to the beautiful aspects when the sun warms your face and your hearts. The sun is your benefactor bringing you happiness and escalates the awareness of the beautiful existence around you. Listen to the chorus at dawn; be aware of the greeting that awaits you. Observe the earth's wedding garments, as she bedecks her body with her coats of many colours and perfumes to assist you in your roles as guardians and to harvest your provisions. Allow your awareness and love to go back to the earth and you will be fulfilling your role and destiny. Allow the spring to come into your lives throughout the year.

The factors of climate and pace of life, together with the effects of the media you allow into your life all tend to bar your way to expressing your awareness of beauty. As you become aware, you allow your flowers of love, compassion and empathy to blossom into full maturity. You become not only aware of sensing the elements of the physical dimension but are able to expand into other states of being and consciousness and are able to appreciate the beautiful aspects of all life and vibrations.

Awareness will also bring you into the moment of **NOW**.

What is this somewhat enigmatic term that many have difficulty in really comprehending? Now does not mean just in this moment of time but it may also mean no w(ay), meaning that there is no other way for doing or being, not in the future or the past, but to be totally in the present. It means to be aware totally in this moment of time. Being in the now is the focusing of your awareness in any given moment.

By exercising your senses more, of hearing, seeing, touching, tasting and feeling you will surely begin to live in the now. Stop and listen to the orchestrations of the feathered fraternity, touch and appreciate the delicate beauty and form of the flowers that have come to bring cheer to your stagnation. Your world is so rich with so many treasures if you would begin to be aware and the richest treasure that you possess is with you **NOW**.

As you become aware of the beauty of creation and feel at one with it, allowing your love to flow in a natural and uninhibited way, then you have touched all that is sacred. Having that total conscious awareness all the time is who you really are.

You have touched the source of your being.

Cultivating your awareness and being grounded in the present moment is such an important part of your development in finding out who you really are, what you really are capable of doing and extending your boundaries into other realities. We become empowered to create change, becoming spiritually strong and secure in the way we feel and are able to radiate that strength and conviction. By extending the normal senses of feeling, hearing, seeing, smell and taste, we can become clairsentient, clairaudient, and clairvoyant.

Stagnation may also lead you into a deeper awareness, for when your whole body is still, your mind may be exercised through imaginative thoughts, such that they may be extended to new boundaries. If you would but try to encourage the use of your senses to a finer degree, your awareness from this would develop your extra-sensory perception. The use of these perceptions is your birthright; it is there for you, with a little effort to be more aware. Humanity has developed such a materialistic outlook that it has forgotten how to connect with life and its deeper significance. It seems that man's only outcome is for the satisfaction of desires and the protection of his securities. On examination of the root cause of his needs it is only the lack of love for himself that he is truly experiencing. Being aware however will bring that love to you. It will bring to you an appreciation of the little things and develop within a reverence for all life. To be aware of your feelings with the trees and animals and to sense and empathise with others will develop your connectedness with all, and with all there is. This is the way to bring love back to you and no longer will you need to search and satisfy your desires and build around you your castles of security.

The next stage for healers is refining their awareness process with people. Many healers just get on with the job after they have tuned in and see what happens, being very aware of what they are doing. Others daydream, perhaps become detached from their performance, or in that state of oneness, in the moment of now, without expectation.

Healers can extend their boundaries by learning to attune to a deeper level and become even more aware, providing useful interaction with their spiritual mentors especially with regard to the conditions requiring attention.

This is a time of connecting, of coming closer to other souls on the journey of self-realisation of the beginnings of brotherhood and sisterhood which will be the way of life and experience in the new age.

All that you do in sharing of the infinite love, wisdom and light, you do in the name of your Creator the great being called love. However, much more than this, as you raise yourself in awareness as beings of light you enhance the love of your Creator. You add to His greatness, this ineffable love. For as you add to the brightness of your own spirit through your experience you also add to the glory of that wonderful being that created the spark of your being.

Over time, I came to realise that there was an interconnection with all life by this creative essence, that we were all part of the same energy that we call God and we were here to share and be that essence. To take that one stage further we are in a sense lesser gods, or gods in the making. We are here in this moment to create what we want to create and having complete free will and freedom of choice to do so and we can use this essence to assist in our creations.

All beings and I mean everyone has an innate awareness, often referred to as psychic ability. It is just that we have forgotten how to use it. It is part of who we are. We are sensitive beings, we can feel things; can access other realities and our intuition. As society has become materialistic through the substance of technology, we have become almost dependant on its existence. The same is happening in the communication revolution. They are excellent tools to expand our creative processes, to save time, a time that we could usefully employ developing those senses that have become dormant.

Not all is lost and we have noticed in the last twenty-five plus years there has been a tremendous surge forward in this reconnection with this latent awareness. Many are openly demonstrating their psychic skills and the media of television and cinema have graced us with expressions of other possibilities and realities. There is a wake-up call going on. There is a shift in consciousness happening now and we are all part of it.

There are those that will continue to deny themselves their abilities that their soul is calling out to them to express who they really are. Their veils of fear and ignorance will always cloud their judgement. In their lack of acceptance and openness there will be an ascendance of mental problems, brought about by their resistance to their own expansion. They will need a special kind of healing of tolerance, compassion and understanding and it will be up to the healers to shine some light on their pathway.

During my wilderness years in the work situation a contractor was using divining rods to locate land drains in a field and surprised me as to his accuracy in locating them. He suggested I might try them and again I was again surprised in my accuracy. I related it to nothing in particular and kept my experience under wraps until some years later on a job I was supervising, a contractor was trying to find a drain for which there were no written records. I volunteered my party piece with hand on my heart and located it exactly where my rods crossed. The word spread of course of the success of the 'experiment' along with all the usual unpleasant comments.

One bright summery day a little more forward in my development, with nothing better to do I took my rods to the back garden and asked mentally if there were any fairies in the garden. I really did not expect a response but those rods crossed very positively. Knowing me, I would not have expected me to be asking such a question but I can say I was at least open to other realities and possibilities. Following through I asked where and the rods pointed to a particular shrub. Going to different parts of the garden and asking the same question confirmed the location. I could not see or feel these non-physical beings, which we could collectively refer to as nature spirits. Some weeks later I asked our friend Kim (whom I have previously referred to) to tune into the shrub area and she channelled information from these beings that their work was finished here and they wanted to move on and would appreciate us channelling our energy for their purpose.

OK so I was away with the fairies but the use of the divining rods and later the pendulum has opened up doorways to awareness for many individuals, including apprehensive teenagers and sceptical husbands.

One woman brought her husband to Peacehaven because she was convinced of his psychic abilities. I took him aside and introduced him to dowsing, then on to sensing energies, fed him with other ideas and possibilities all in a short space of a few hours. Within a few months, he was visiting stone circles, dowsing for energy and ley lines and eventually developed a direct communication link with his guide.

I have found that men particularly when introduced to extra sensory work by way of practical applications, find it more easily acceptable and not to jump in at the deep end with something that is not tangible.

Crucial ingredients necessary for development:

> **A** wareness –observation of self and nature
> **P** ractice – including prayer, devotion and ritual
> **P** erception – widening the vision
> **L** ove – of self and cleansing of emotions
> **E** xpression – allowing it
>
> **P** erseverance – keep trying
> **I** ntention – focus with clarity
> **E** xpectation – use the imagination

AWARENESS

Oh my God do teach me
To open up my heart,
From a bud to full flower
To be a very part.

A part of the universe
Unique in esteem,
But full of love and wonderment
Of life's unending dream.

Allow the spark you gave me
To expand my very being,
To grow in love to Christ-hood
For my soul to be far-seeing.

To see the beauty of creation
Your love in every soul,
In saint and sinner together
Each and every role.

Give me God your guidance
Through the living of more strife,
Lift my mind to greater things
Through the seasons of my life.

Let me feel your sunshine
The warmth of love supreme,
And the patter of the raindrops
Even while I dream.

Let me feel your presence
In every thing I do,
Take my body in awareness
In your loving nature too.
Forgive me God my nature

Of my little erring ways,
Help purify this vehicle
And everything it says.

Open up my heart so wide
So they can see that all it brings,
Of love so clear it has for you
And the praise this singer sings.

CHAPTER 14

The Shift

Be still and know,
that I am your friend always by your side,
I am there to help you and always be your guide.
Through the times of trials and the seasons of your life,
I am there to give you strength to take away your strife.
So share with me these moments when you need a hand to hold,
with My heart to ever warm you to keep you in My fold.

At this time of the evolution of the planet earth, our spiritual mentors inform us that there is a great influx or a pouring of spiritual energy over the earth. This energy, symbolised by the Aquarian spirit pouring the water of life from the urn of eternity is a gift from the universe, the life force, that essence we call God. It is bringing forward a new and greater awareness at this time, a raising of consciousness to different levels of awareness which will help each individual (should they so choose) realise his/her true identity and their relationship with each other, the earth and the creative essence of all life.

For many there will also be an intensive process of searching and discovering. There will be personal transformations in this awakening when these aspects of the life force will be channelled through many people, as many energetic forms from different vibrations come closer to the physical vibration. As people become aware and tap into this wonderful energy of their angelic guardians they will create a bridgehead to their higher or christed self, moving even closer to the source and embracing unconditional love.

There are other forms of reality - mental, emotional and most importantly spiritual. It is one thing to live in the physical reality but not to the exclusion of other non-physical realities. It is good if you are able to discover and consider these other realities, play with them, deal with them in your mind but do so with detachment. The outworking of the exploration into other regions of life will expunge the need to have that experience in physical reality. Humanity is working on all levels of being

119

*just as your spirit is part of many vibrations and levels. Learn to accept
these states, these realities, work with them with an involvement but detach
yourself from them and let go.*

*We are of fellowship of light - your brothers in a realm of non-physical
space, not just the universal space, but also the space in which thought
resides. There is such beauty in this space that you would call the mind
of God. Enter that space away from your own limitations and you will
experience the thoughts we share with you.*

*There are many who are reaching out to make that link with the
source. The energy of your beings has yet to be refined to receive these
vibrations. Practice more of the deep breathing and this will connect you
with your true self. It is difficult to categorise the levels of the origins of these
thoughts but there are parallel dimensions to your own. As your perspective
is towards spiritual love and the Christ light which may also bring power
and wisdom, there are also perspectives towards power and wisdom in their
own right. All these are aspects of the source to which we all strive.*

*The power to perceive another reality is within all. It is part of human
inheritance that has been lost or has become dormant, as the human mind
has allowed itself to become enmeshed in material existence but it is still
there, as another sense to be used to enable that connection with the Christ
status, the whole and the inter-dimensional part of their existence.*

*The quality of perception will become more apparent in the growth
of awareness in recognition of the little things instead of plain acceptance.
Examine what you see. Feel the energy of vibration and the feeling it
conveys.*

What is Channelling?

A Channel is a conduit or way through which something may
flow, carried, or transmitted. Just as healing flows or is the transmission
of energy or life force through individuals, then other aspects of that
life force are also be transmitted. In scientific terms none of these other
aspects are objective in that they cannot generally be measured or
proved but it can be quite a convincing experience for the channel and
the recipient.

During the nineteenth and twentieth centuries, mediumship was
the term used for channelling especially with the advent of spiritualism,

whereby a person was able to tune into the energy of a discarnate entity. This process of fine-tuning was by a process known as trance, which also encompassed the qualities of clairvoyance and clairaudience. Usually it was necessary for people to train to develop these particular gifts through perhaps years of meditation and spiritual practices. Now it is not so necessary to experience development in this way since many souls entering the earth's dimension unfold naturally and at a quicker pace in step with their spiritual growth.

Channelling is like opening a box and allowing the sunshine from outside to pour into your life. In this process, you are tuning into other frequencies of being that will enable you and assist you to make the greatest spiritual growth in this lifetime. This fine-tuning does not always come about by a communication link but in fact has always existed, the results producing inspired works of art, literature, music and poetry. We have only to read the scriptures of various religions to find with great frequency, reference to prophets who were able to contact and relay information from discarnate beings some of which were interpreted as God or angels.

Everyone has the capacity to channel to a degree, depending on their awareness and by opening hearts and minds and mentally agreeing to attune, receive, communicate and aligning their energies, the door is always open.

What are the advantages of Channelling?

Channelling gives you the opportunity to discover and express the God presence within and learning to trust that. This will enable you to look at life from a higher and wider perspective and an understanding of oneness with creation. Perceptions will broaden and awareness will deepen, teaching you about life, giving you empowerment, self-respect, self-discipline and changing the way you think.

By shifting your mind to an expanded state of awareness, there will be access to a higher universal wisdom and information and by allowing yourself to communicate from this source you will grow in grace, power and love. Others will be inspired by your example and grow through your experience which will in turn guide them into a greater awareness of their potential.

CHILD OF THE SPIRIT

Child of the spirit come home to me
When you are at one with liberty,
To fulfil your dreams and prove your worth
In different realms within the earth.

Child of the spirit lift up your heart
Gather the lessons to make a start,
Open your mind and be aware
Of heaven and earth you make there.

Come carry your load and share with all
With those who come and hear the call
Oh child of the spirit come home to me
Hear the call to set you free.

What is wisdom but the total knowledge and understanding of that knowledge from experience. It is not just a knowledge of that experience, a registration of that experience on the psyche, but a deeper collective understanding of why that experience occurred and what particular qualities of spirit have evolved.

The wisdom gained in life is a very personal journey and may not always apply to a similar condition in another's reality, but that wisdom is also there to help them with their own perceptions. Your wisdom is not a substitute for their experience but merely as guidance to assist in their own store of wisdom. All wisdom, like the other attributes of the source, is part of the essence and as such is in all things, thus wisdom also belongs to and is available for all.

There are many wise beings with wisdom to share. Through their own evolutionary process, they are able to connect also to the wisdom of their higher self, either consciously or unconsciously. In turn that aspect of their being forms a bridge with the universal mind of the creative essence we call God, which is the source of infinite wisdom.

For each individual if you so desire, channelling is the doorway to constant love, perfect understanding and unending compassion. By forming a bridge to other realities, it can release a tremendous potential and allow us to express our full divinity. We just have to make that shift to extend the boundaries of our physical reality. We have to open our box.

Forms of Channelling

When channelling, reference is invariably made to a being communicating or relating information from an expanded state of awareness either unconsciously or consciously.

Unconscious channelling occurs when the person is in deep trance. Effectively this means that the spirit of the person has temporarily vacated the body while in a sleep/unconscious state and another entity speaks through the individual, often with different vocal characteristics. At the end of the communication the entity withdraws, the spirit re-enters and the person awakes having no recollection of what the entity said. This system of channelling rarely occurs and it relies on implicit trust on the part of the sitter and is generally an agreed contract set up before incarnation takes place.

Conscious channelling means just that. Each person is conscious while relaying information, although feeling as though they are on another cloud. They are able to remember most or only parts of what they have related. As more advanced beings are entering the world at this time it is not thought necessary that trance states are required since more are able to access the source of their being and bring it into their consciousness. At the conscious end of this spectrum, we also have clairvoyance, clairaudience, precognition, telepathy and other inspired creativities.

With what realities are we connecting?

There are many realities out there in the universe as there are around us. Just as we are in the main unaware of their existence, those that dwell in their own space may well prefer it that way but because of their perceptions, they are able to find it a little easier than us to transverse these different realities.

Based on the law of attraction that like attracts like, you will consciously be able to connect to that level which corresponds to your spiritual development. As the thoughts and vibrations of the individual increase then the communication link will be from a higher level.

There are many levels or dimensions within your own space, all interwoven, the higher dimensions or vibrations being on a much vaster scale because there are no limitations. There are difficulties that persist in your limited world and that includes fine-tuning into other vibrations of existence but these difficulties also occur transforming energies and thoughts into your mind frame and personalities. Your personality egos are required at times with your consent and that of your higher consciousness, to relay a particular message, whether it is for a general shake-up, encouragement, or to provide love and grace, and may be verbalised or expressed in written form. Be assured also that as a person begins to channel that they are not necessarily all connecting to the same point of reference or the same source of that entity, but one of the multi-dimensional aspects within the many dimensions.

As your lives are facets of your higher self, each personality brings lustre to the diamond of your christed beings, so also there are many aspects of our being, unlimited in dimensional terms that may still carry a fragment of our many personalities. Try therefore through exercise, patience and tolerance, to attain those heights where you think we are, raise your vibrations to the greater truth that awaits you. Please discern all that you hear and read. Take even these words within your own hearts for its truth, judge not another because of what they say is not resonating with you, because they are trying with love to make their best connection, love them for what they do. You will know their space and that those others will also perceive your space.

There is a sea of consciousness of truth everywhere accessible by all according to their own truth. You attract that truth according to your desire, your own space and your own vibration and you attract that aspect of another being that relates to your own truth. Truth is relative to the being that works for it.

The purity of channelling is also relative to that being that becomes open to channel. No channel is perfect in your frequencies of vibration except perhaps a handful that have come close to mastering your limitations and they are able to access closer to the source and can handle and adjust to the finer vibrations. That is not to say that all other utterances and words are untruths. There are many that speak great truths from their position and from the plane they have accessed. There is in truth one truth through all consciousness but that truth may become a little cloudy at times, so rise above the clouds into the pure light of truth.

Most people are able to connect to the astral levels, referred to as the fourth dimension. This is the level souls pass through immediately after passing from the physical reality that we call death. In the astral realms, there are many levels and each being will 'migrate' to that level according to its spiritual development. 'In my house there are many mansions' and each will go to the 'mansion' deserving of them corresponding to their emotional or mental state of mind.

At the lower levels is that reality that we would loosely term hell, although from a spirit's perspective hell is that place called earth! The truth is heaven and hell is where you choose to make it. These tend to be the areas where there are lost souls unable to move forward due to unresolved issues. It is here that many groups make contact through rescue circles. Some become stuck in their emotional or mental state at the time of passing or because of the trauma in which they passed and through the group they are encouraged to move on to happier climes. Those that use the life force in a negative way will reap the appropriate reward and unfortunately may still cling to the physical reality of earth. In these circumstances, they may hook themselves into the energy field of a like-minded person and continue the wallowing of their negativity. In the same way, those beings that have led an addictive life may continue their addictions by proxy.

If these beings refuse assistance being offered for their own good and will not listen to the help, it is unfortunately necessary to let them stew in their own juice until such time that they are ready to move on. For many psychically undeveloped people that have been 'hooked' by an undesirable entity, it is possible to dispose of this extra garbage. There is an unwritten challenge in the universe that carries with it great power. Whenever one feels uncomfortable with the presence of a spirit entity, you should challenge it three times with the phrase 'Do you come in the light and love of God?' There should be an unequivocal 'Yes'. If there is any doubt, especially with the third answer tell them to sling their hook.

As you increase your awareness and develop your abilities to channel, you will attract to you many energies and entities. As moths are attracted to the light, then these beings become attracted to your light. Some are attracted because they can see the potential for their growth some come to enhance your light into a greater light because of your desire to do so.

There are those entities also who are intent on being manipulative, wishing to use your energies for their own devious means.

It is of this group that you should be particularly aware, especially if in the course of your development you display the emotions of fear or desire for your own importance. You are encouraged to challenge such beings if you feel unsettled by their presence and you may do this by an exhibition of your love. Three times, you would ask if they come in the light and love of God and three times you would have an affirmative answer. If this is not so, you would dispatch them with your love. The laws are written so that beings not of your vibration cannot withstand the energies so emitted and will depart. This should be exercised with love and without the display of emotions, fear and anger.

A little extra ammunition you can shoot their way is for them a little of that 'hell' they have created for themselves:

L for **Light** to because they need it in their darkness,
L for **Laughter** because they have forgotten happiness,
L for **Love** because their hearts have grown cold,
all wrapped up with a prayer.

Some schools of development place great emphasis on protection and there are certain rituals adopted like opening and closing the energy centres and surrounding you in a bubble of golden light. Protection implies that there is something to be afraid of, so fear will create more fear and like will attract like which will derive sustenance from that fear. The antidote of fear is love and if you work on the vibration of love that is all the protection you will need. If you are not entirely happy with that then adopt any method that makes you feel happy. As an alternative, you can always try garlic!

Fear is a key to your enfoldment because of the doors that it may unlock to bring balance into your lives. How can you know that the positive attributes of goodness and Godliness are good, unless from your perspective you have a yardstick with which to measure them? You need such a measuring device because of the limitations in your frequency of vibration. How indeed can you know ultimate happiness unless you have experienced the depths of despair?

Fear provides a means for you to assimilate and understand the truth. Understanding and acceptance of fear will bring a balance to your lives. It is not necessary to wear the robes of fear in order to learn, although some have to, to restore their balance, but it is more important to understand fear and its vibration. It is what fear can do to the energy of all life streams, how it can smother and similarly affect growth patterns and evolvement that should be understood.

The antidote of fear is love and knowing that the protective mantle of love will turn away fear and provide all necessary comfort in such times of adversity.

Adversity appears at your doorstep when there are lessons you need to adsorb into your being, to understand that experience, to learn the antidote and the attraction of that attribute to bring about your wholeness. So understand that as adverse conditions attract fear, an opportunity also presents itself to attract love. As easy as it is to follow one path, one can also follow another, although going uphill, and you can feel lighter as you ascend the upward path, leaving the baggage of fear at the crossroads.

Most people that are inherently 'good' migrate to the higher astral levels, to their little piece of heaven or the one they have created. From their new perspective, they can see things differently; how negative emotions and mental attitudes can have a debilitating effect on one's development and also how the lessons learnt from those experiences can be so beneficial. These souls do much to encourage those still in the earth realm and can see better windows of opportunity that would be forthcoming, without interfering or being judgemental in material lifestyles. The wisdom emanating from this reality is generally good but is not necessarily of the highest order.

Higher wisdom may be accessed from what is loosely termed the fifth dimension and above. These are the mental levels and are the 'homes' of more enlightened souls, our guides, teachers and philosophers of the great white brotherhood.

Everyone has some form of spiritual guidance from one of the many dimensions of non-physical existence. Most of us have this guidance from a higher reality and it is there throughout our lives, to guide, nurture, inspire and protect us when we ask for it and it is for our higher good. They are not there to run our lives for us, they are there merely to teach and support and in no way are they allowed to alter our destiny or to remove a problem if it involves our spiritual growth. These evolved beings have incarnated on earth probably through many incarnations, have earned the right to guide and desired the experience of guiding for their own future evolvement.

If for instance, you deliberately did something wrong it would be something you have created and it would be for you to un-create or take responsibility for the consequences, but the support is always there.

We also have the service of doorkeepers, who provide protection and in their past lives may have been indigenous natives where vigilance and strength are developed qualities. Their specialty is dealing with lower energies or earthbound spirits that may try to sink their hooks

BY MY SIDE

An angel came by just then
and touched my mantle glow,
it surged my being with its embrace
and love began to flow.
My love poured forth from hallowed cup
from an unending store,
and even though while I slept
there was always chance for more.
I followed my lighted friend
to many realms untrod,
but ever closer do I believe
to the force that I call God.
Many mansions did I visit
to many sights unseen,
touching sight of heaven
in the places I had been.
We walked and talked of many things
of love and what it meant,
of all its diverse avenues
and why to earth we are sent.
It seems to me we experience
who we really are
as expressions of divinity
making contact with our star.
That star is our sweet essence
our ability to create
a tiny part of heaven
on earth without the hate.

I have come to love my angel
whom I know is my best friend,
one who guides my pathway
to my journeys end.
I know at times I've given grief
through choices that I make
instead of listening to the wisdom
and causing ripples in my wake.
I do appreciate the guidance
I know its always there
if I just stop and listen
and try to be aware.
I'm calling now my faithful friend
to help me change my ways
that I might be an enabler
of God throughout my days.
So dear friend I bear no guilt
for all that's gone before
but I do regret the hurt I've caused
perhaps to settle a score.
Judgement neither do I make
because of their closed door
but I pray one day they'll open
and see what's in their store.
Help me friend to release them
to say its all O.K.
as God would say 'Forgiveness
is freedom along your way'

into unwary individuals. From time to time we also receive the services of other spiritual personnel that are there temporarily to channel special qualities through the recipient.

Another vibration closely associated with the earth but are not part of it are the celestial or angelic realms. These formless beings although given wings (to differentiate them from other entities) work more directly with the Christ light in their respective fields of teaching, healing, protection, truth, wisdom etc. If your aspirations are to channel the Christ light then guidance may be from this level.

Once the principles of the existence of other realities are accepted and if it has not been a natural development to be in communication with spiritual guidance then the next step is making that shift. For some it may be difficult because of the walls of their box are difficult to climb. No one can do it for you but others can share their experience.

Each vibration resonates with its own truth, from its own perspective, but that may not necessarily be the complete truth.

If it were possible to graduate the progression of communication and information, it would approximate to the following sequence.

Initially there may be information appertaining to the channel and others to gain your interest and momentum. The next levels would be predictive in nature, appealing somewhat to your emotional natures. These will help you develop your powers of discernment and bring balance to your beings, and hopefully responsibility with regard to your creations for your future roles. Teachings follow concerning your emotions, learning to let go of the accumulated dross of your existence and advice on how to separate yourself from your attachments.

Then we come into the stream of mental mind bending of new concepts, ideologies and looking at limitation from a universal viewpoint. Expansion of your mind to see the whole picture of past, present and future from the now point is the opportunity that may be presented and available for each one of you. Do not be in haste for this eventuality, it will disorientate your mind if it is not ready. The whole process must be gradual. Each must open as flowers to absorb the light that waits. Know that some flowers have the resilience and strength to assume an abundance of light and others by intent of the grace of their delicate nature are slower to open to the grandeur that is theirs. All have that potential to open to full blossom.

As your mind expands, as your heart expands with love also, then you will come to know and be an expression of the universal mind of God. Know that in that mind there is an ocean of truth, each receives an aspect of truth according to their own understanding, where they are and what they need to restore balance to their being. All is under direction of the universal mind.

CHAPTER 15

The Leap

Be still and know,
that in searching for me constantly through the stillness of your mind,
in being patient for those moments that you will surely find;
my outstretched hand to guide you, my voice to calm your fears,
my love to always warm you, to carry you through the years.

Placing your trust in something that you may feel is the result of an overactive imagination is like standing on top of a cliff and taking one small step forward. But it does not have to be a confrontational experience or a fearful one because there is nothing to fear only your own limitations. If you would like and intend to make that leap then it is always desirable to have the assistance of someone you can trust and has experience of communication with spirit.

What preparation is required to channel.

There are a number of attributes and qualities that need to be developed to become a clear and open channel. One of the most difficult areas is learning to *focus* and concentrate without expectation, of keeping your desires, demands or wondering what out of the way information is coming next. They are a natural development in the course of learning to channel especially consciously, since the fear of saying something stupid in front of an audience is always in the forefront of your mind.

Learning to *trust* in its various aspects is another obstacle on the course. Trusting in yourself and acknowledging that you are in full control of any situation builds the confidence and stimulates caution. You are able at any time to stop what you are doing if you feel that something is trying to control you and it enables you to be cautious and wary of energies if you are unsure. In the case of conscious channelling trusting does not mean surrendering body, mind and spirit. It means leaving your mind *open* to possibilities, exercising *detachment* and until you feel comfortable, monitor your feelings and the communications you are receiving. Deep trance however does mean total surrender but this is not something you learn in this life, it is a contract you made with your guide before you came here whereby your soul has already received the required 'training'.

Those communications do need **expression**. In the early stages of development with most people, the communications tend to be of a more personal nature and do not always find an outward expression but if the intent is that the information is to be shared then the way the information is interpreted requires **monitoring** by the agencies supplying the information. If symbols are transmitted to the channel, then the channel puts their own interpretation on the symbolism using their own vocabulary and it may not be quite what is trying to be conveyed so other words or symbols are used to elucidate the message. The **emotions** of the channel can also colour the communication link and again detachment is the key. The most challenging situation is sharing information clairvoyantly or otherwise with your nearest and dearest, when your communication echoes exactly what you have been feeling. It is then you have to express what you receive and detach, let it go and wait for the results. Not to smugly say 'I told you so' but to help your own confidence in your ability.

If you are **enthusiastic** and **willing** to learn to be a channel, can develop **patience** to interpret, patience with your own understanding and development then being a channel can be fun. You are under no duress or pressure, you can turn it on whenever you like, like a water tap, the constancy of supply always being there. Enjoy what you do and keep a sense of humour whenever possible. One particular clairvoyant medium who's performance was a pleasure, kept his vibrations at the highest level by laughing his way through his own jokes and the guidance given and enraptured his audiences and congregations every time.

If you need a **communication** link then **ask** for it and ask for the highest guidance possible. It is always there. It always has been. It is only us that get in the way, our ego personality that always seems to know what is best. Learn to spend time alone, to **attune** to the energies at your disposal. Daydream if you will to develop your intuitive guidance, examine the difference between the thoughts that are the product of your own mind and those thoughts that pop in unexpectedly.

As with all forms of channelling **love** is the key to success. Loving without conditions or strings will clarify and purify any information or effort. Love is the bridge between worlds, dimensions and other states of being. It is the essence, the glue, bringing us all together.

I am that aspect of love that you call glue -the sticky stuff, that which enables you to make a connection, one with another. I am the energy of attraction. Because all energy has mind, just as you are energy and you have mind also. So why cannot an abstract energy also have a mind?

I am in all things, attached to desire, compassion, possession, avarice -I am free. I come when you ask to glue your feelings, cement your emotions but I am at my most expressive form when you love unconditionally. I am like rubber, stretched when there is a pull of negative energy but when I am merged with unconditional love, my potential is maximised.

The Connection

Nearly everyone has at some time has experienced the goose pimple feeling when someone has just walked over their grave or when the hair on the back of the head has stood on end. This usually indicates that some form of spiritual energy has come into that person's energy field and may be an expression of their higher self, their guide, helper, deceased relative or friend, or some other spirit being who wishes to be known or has a message to convey. When you become a little more sensitive, while meditating for instance, you may experience a gentle touching your face or even someone holding your hand. Because of a general lack of awareness of these matters, the goose pimples are directly associated to fear on the part of the individual.

When your guide wants to make their presence known, they will make their connection and transmit with repetition a few words. The transmission in the first instance feels like a telepathic communication, the implantation of a thought and a focus is required to allow that thought to expand to receive the full context of the message. It eventually leads on to the scenario where you are talking to yourself like the time you entertained your imaginary friend as a child. As clairaudience develops, you may experience yourself listening as though someone is talking to you directly.

In the early stages of development, you deliberate trying to summon the courage to speak out, but change your mind because you do not want to make a fool of yourself. They are very patient beings but then they start pulling your strings. You find your leg starts to twitch, your nose itches incessantly or you develop some other mild affliction. It is their way of reminding you what you have agreed to do and to take that leap into the unknown. Can you imagine them having a party when you make that leap of faith?

When you decided to come into your reality, you agreed to demonstrate and channel the various aspects of the Creator. You decided that you would try to express your creativity in its many forms and you owe it to yourself to do this. There are difficulties you endure as you become trapped in your materialistic reality and how the ego assumes its role. Your fears are understood and how you lack courage when embarking on a new project. When you become awakened to the project of universal life, there will be apprehension, fears and of course the courage one needs to move forward and channel this essence called love in its multiple forms.

Verbalising in public is one of the most difficult and may express the greatest fear of being a fool and not knowing what you are going to say. It is a matter of trusting and that trust will overcome such fears. More importantly, you made a contract of sorts prior to your present incarnation to perform certain tasks, including perhaps channelling vibrations in their various forms. If in your awareness you refuse to demonstrate your creativity because of your hangups, you will still have those feelings of inadequacy when you move on from your present reality.

Within each of you is a spark of the creative essence and it is your right to allow that essence to realise its full potential. You have also been given freewill in all matters and that includes whether or not you wish that essence to express itself. When, however, you know you are capable, that in your heart you have agreed to do this, the burden you carry will be heavier. Your awareness will bring you into aspects of mastery necessary for your evolution and it will make you aware of the burdens you carry. Mastery is after all surrendering your burdens to God and this will give you your freedom to express your creativity. If these words bring forward an emotional negative response then you will know to what we refer.

We all make mistakes. It is our way of learning and we all make them on the pathway to development. We may hesitate as we try to relay the information given to us. That is all right. We may inadvertently say the wrong word or are a little confused. That is all right. These things happen. We are all on a learning curve and have to start somewhere and because of so many unknowns and that we are still trying to monitor the thoughts we are expressing we get in the way. With practice, these become minor difficulties as you learn to trust your source and open your heart.

When this love flows freely, that is without effort, then it is coming from the source of all knowingness, all beingness. It is perfection. You are allowing your higher presence to flow through you, which is the perfection all beings in all dimensions strive.

When a being in your dimension is flowing with this love, you will know it and you will feel it. You will know and feel their vibrations and the energy charge they have left behind in any space they have filled. Others that are sufficiently sensitive will feel and be attracted to those vibrations from a distance and will naturally home in to that energy because of their desire to fulfill the hunger that lies within.

Love is being without effort. It is a natural desire to give, to share, to be part of the ALL. It is surrender of the ego to all there is and expressing and being all there is. It is being of the flow of life, allowing it to pass through, and allowing it to flow back to the ALL.

Love has no boundaries, no limitations, it is a fluid like liquid gold and where there is a space it will flow into it.

All those that walk in the light of love are truly Holy people. They are truly hole-y people, like sieves they allow their love essence to flow through them and out. A truly holy person is a large hole, an empty vessel, where all the life force, all the love and wisdom of the universal consciousness may flow through and out without restriction.

The more your heart is opened the more love can flow through it and when you speak from the heart your inhibitions and fears dissolve in the warmth and radiance of the light that burns there.

As you become overshadowed by the discarnate guidance it is common to experience changes in breathing patterns, shallower or deeper breathing, differences in temperature in different parts of the body and other energy changes. Part of this reaction is the overshadowing process as the entity is adjusting to your energy system and part is the release of inhibitions and fears in accommodating another energy into your space. In a deeper trance/unconscious state the voice may change as the entity takes more control giving a decidedly convincing act that there is someone else there and in rarer instances the face of the medium may transfigure or appear to resemble the face of entity who is speaking.

It should be emphasised that when guides, angels, helpers, or other discarnate beings are working through their human channels they have no desire to create any fears or intention to control. All the fears we experience are through our own ignorance and lack of understanding. Our fears are our own creations. Comfort of the channel is of prime importance: comfort of the physical body, mentally with the being communicating and emotionally with those that listen, being with ourselves, where we are, who we are and what we are doing.

You may find or feel that your benign guide or helper is an angel, a North American Indian, Chinese philosopher, or intergalactic traveller. So many get wrapped up in an egoistic dilemma, traumatised by the ostentatious importance of having such an associate. The last thing they desire is any form of idolatry on your part or to be worshipped like gurus, they would say they are there to serve and in that service, they are serving themselves, their own advancement and the source of all being. The guise you associate with them may have been the energy they developed in that incarnation which they bring to you at this time. As you develop, you may feel inclined to refer to them as, 'my source' or 'my guidance', which they would be quite happy with since we are all from the 'source' and all gratitude should of course be sent in that direction.

The Landing

After a channelling session, channellers and mediums will experience different reactions to the event that has just taken place irrespective of their conscious state. There may be tiredness or a drained feeling, which in part is due to a resistance to the channelling in the early development, or a feeling of being energised, spaced out or disorientated. All these sensations are quite common at various stages of development and depend on the state of consciousness of the channel.

There will be apprehensions and doubts at first, whether all was a result of an over active imagination, or if you had cribbed it from a book you had been reading. It is good to read to release your own innate understanding and often the theme that is selected, will give you that comfort. In your progression there will be introductions to other themes and deviations. (Some of them have probably been psychologists, diplomats or even politicians). Discrepancies will occur in the information given but it should be remembered that all this (certainly conscious) channelled wisdom depends on the intellect, spiritual understanding and awareness of the individual channel. As with any information, exercise discernment against the individual's sense of truth and what feels right.

With the connection to this greater awareness there comes peace and contentment, a sense of 'going home', of reaching out to the source from which you have come. A butterfly has emerged from the cocoon. You have jumped out of your box.

Like having a new toy, any involvement with spiritual disciplines will carry you away to dizzy heights and you may feel as high as a kite. Perspectives may be temporarily lost, together with imbalances giving way to erratic behaviour. In this regard, connecting with spiritual energy and opening up too quickly can be very unbalancing and mentally confusing. It is like planting a sapling and giving it deluges of water. The soil is washed away leaving the roots open and unprotected.

To moderate this inpouring of energy, it is important to take care of diet, sleep and to participate in menial tasks like gardening, cleaning and washing up. By connecting to the earth and water in this way will provide grounding by 'having your feet on the ground'.

The Song of the Universe

Contained within the body of the light there are many, many vibrations each with their own groups. It is rather like the colour spectrum, each colour is a different rate of vibration and there are many colours. Each colour has its own particular purpose to fulfil in the order of the cosmos.

You may be aware of the meanings of different colours but the subject is much more complex than this. Sometimes there is a blending of vibrations of colour required for a special purpose. It is rather like a musical composition, each note is a colour vibration and makes little sense on its own but combined with all the other notes the composition or outcome would be so beautiful. Again take that note away from the composition and its beauty can be lost.

There are also countless compositions being composed in the same moment in time. The mind in its limited human form cannot comprehend the magnitude of the operation of the cosmos.

Listen to the silence. Listen to the music that surrounds you, the music of the spiritual realms; the music of the voice beside you - inside you. There is so much of this music pouring over the earth at this time. Listen hard to the songs, to the music that is played and you will feel and hear the vibrations sent down to you. So much is lost because so little is exercised to raise your vibrations, to receive these beautiful inspirations. Listen. Just listen.

CHAPTER 16

God And All That (Is)

Be still and know,
I am your essence I am in many things
my spark I send on forward to shine the light it brings.
That light is my beginning starting life anew,
creating yet another world - expanding me and you.

Healing is all about letting go; letting go of self imposed limitations, letting go of expectations from ourselves and others, letting go of old hurts and new ones as they arise. It is letting go of the crap pile that has been placed on our shoulders from the minute we screamed into the world, including all the stuff we brought with us that we need to deal with. To be more effective healers we need to compost our garbage and our own process of accessing and sharing the divine energy will do that. To be healers that are more effective and to make a difference to this world means jumping out of the comfort zone of your own little box.

This also includes letting go of our perceptions and limitations of who we are and letting go of our perceptions as to whom and what god is.

During the centuries of the Piscean and previous epochs, various individuals carried the mantle of authority under the guise of priests and shamans. It is some of the people through their religious doctrines and belief systems, who have undermined the minds of the populace by domination and subjugation by playing and preying on blind ignorance.

Overall, there has always been a desire for humans to have a belief system, an awareness of something greater other than themselves. With a shift in consciousness from ideologies and belief systems that is happening at this time, there is a realisation that you are greater than you perceive yourself to be.

This has resulted by an inherent awareness of a connection with something greater, like a newly born child knowing and feeling the detachment when removed from its mother. As man incarnates there is a separation of sorts from a greater part and the churches have used this concept to control 'lost' beings to surrender their power to them. That is not to say that was wrong. We cannot judge what someone believed to be right at the time. Humanity as a whole may have needed those evolutionary steps in place for their understanding to mature to this moment in time.

This moment in time is the most powerful moment of your life. A moment when you can turn around, turn upside down and inside out your mental concepts of these beliefs however they may appear. You are not discarding your belief systems but merely changing their method of application just by releasing your expectations of outcomes and letting go of limitations. It is all right to have a belief system or religion if you wish, accepting those tenets regarding morality and social structure. However, as an individuated being in this moment to place your own interpretation on what all this means is all down to expanding your perceptions and releasing your limitations about what god is now and how you perceive god. It is about stepping out of your box.

As people become more self-empowered, they are tending to move away from a personalised god that is a vengeful being dishing out judgements according to his will. Those who have moved into this space of self-empowerment, feel and know that the continuance and acceptance of such ideas are not the way forward.

In present definitions, god is becoming to be accepted as the life force, which permeates everything from the amoeba to the universe. This definition will be the only one that explains what god is.

Let us now look at some of the misconceptions we have about God. We have been guided by the idea that god is a personalised being, mainly because people cannot get their head around the idea of God being an intangible energy. To worship something that has not some form is beyond the normal and limited thought processes, which is why we have found substitutes such as Jesus, Mohammed, Buddha etc. who exemplified the essence of what god is. One is no better than the other is, they had all made their connection to their essence but each had to formulate it in such a way for their period of history.

Now a greater part of the consciousness of humanity is reaching out, expanding, removing barriers as to who they are and in turn to who or what god is.

God is not superman. God is not a being. God is not a spirit. The word 'god' in fact limits god to what is, when in fact god is an infinite benevolent life force, without limitation, that is the matrix of our universe.

God is the Essence.

If god is an energy, without gender, without form and is the life force, then it does not need to judge, does not need or want anything, does not have emotions, does not get hurt. However, the essence of what God is does have a consciousness - the universal mind, which is non-static, forever changing, forever expanding due to the knowledge, wisdom and understanding that all life feeds into the essence.

Some years ago when I awakened to my somewhat intermittent connection with other dimensions and realities, I gathered some thoughts together to express my truth at that time.

IN THE BEGINNING ...

Many millions of years ago in that existence before time, our creator, that force of love decided that to enhance its nature it would expand itself. With that expansion would come growth and with that growth, knowledge and over time wisdom and love from the experience of knowing.

Our creator decided that to feel that love reflected back on itself it would create a paradise with a fixed space/time environment. That paradise would grow with all its life forms, detached from the source yet still connected. In the experience of that reality through the freedom of will and choice, it was expected that the experience of life would be returned to the creator with gratitude and love.

Thus it was that the earth was created for that paradise.

The creator decreed that it should sustain a diverse variety of life forms, which would evolve in harmony and peace for a period. The earth evolved into a third dimensional reality and it was the first time in the history of the universe that perfection was perceived in such a dense state.

This was all part of an experiment of love, so that love could

143

through the action of free will, be given back to the universal mind. The outcome or conclusion of this experiment was not known, although a particular outcome was desired. Nowhere in the universe, would there be such a diversity of life, colour and vibration, which could provide the joy, harmony, growth and love from that experience. It was a garden of paradise.

However, all gardens need gardeners.

A call went out to all the civilisations in the universe for volunteers to take part in this experiment, to tend this earth paradise and to enhance harmonious relationships with the diversity of life forms. Complete freedom would be given to those volunteers to recognise their own divinity and to be creative within this paradise. This call went out to those aspects of itself that were working within the various rays or attributes of the creator such as power, wisdom, love, purity, truth, devotion, freedom, to bring that aspect of the creator into this third dimensional reality.

These aspects were non-physical beings, radiating that resplendent quality of the creator. Such was their joy in the new environment that they condensed themselves within it.

These beings wanted to enhance other beings from the universe and procreated with them as well as the species developing upon the earth. Their desires for the physical reality became more abundant and in so doing, they created a greater distance from their origins and developed personality egos and detachment from their higher or Christ selves, which brought about violation of the Universal Laws. The bodies became dense, the soul entrapped by desire and subsequent emotions that became part of the individual. In the third dimension there is always decay and regeneration and to this fell the bodies of humankind. The soul on completion of a physical existence felt a need to incarnate again because of desire of the material, which could provide the opportunity for growth, both positive and negative. Therefore, these volunteers became trapped in the wheel of rebirth, oblivious of their destiny and the work they had volunteered to carry out. They had now also to learn to balance the physical and spiritual parts of their being in order to maintain contact with their origins. Memories of the connection with their divinity were erased and no assistance could be given because of the edict of freewill given to all, only that to receive

144

help it must be requested.

Thus came the fall of humanity. In the freedom of their physicality, their gardening instincts were neglected; the earth was abused, raped and plundered for greed and lust. The earth became polluted and the experiment seemed doomed to failure, but all was not yet lost.

An edict was given that humanity should receive a wake-up call.

That time is now happening.

...AND NOW

This may only be a story constructed from an overactive imagination but the elements may not be so far from the truth. We may now consider the concept of the essence at some stage deciding to expand itself to extend its boundaries of consciousness by splitting itself up in myriads of energy and sending them out into space. Each one of those energy patterns, which may be loosely termed our higher or christed self could then fragment its energy into smaller 'parcels' investigating different realities and dimensions. As an analogy consider the role of a grandparent wanting to know everything there is to know in the world, then that grandparent would send out its sons, daughters and grandchildren everywhere to have all sorts of experiences and come back and share the experience. Whilst the offspring are expanding their horizons, the grandparent is doing likewise but on a greater scale.

Some of those energy patterns or parcels may consciously work together working with a particular attribute of the essence such as wisdom, power, love and truth thereby enhancing that quality to a greater degree.

There is within the universal mind a hierarchical expression, which all may have access to if the qualities of their creative essence have reached the purest form. There is also the one point, the alpha and omega, the one point, which has no description, no boundaries, it just is. The hierarchical structures stream out from the universal mind through all dimensions even to your present states of being. There is always guidance available at all levels to provide you with the impetus for your growth.

Each level of understanding is right for you as you open to greater possibilities, as your consciousness desires to be part of a greater expression. Each level is a test, not to achieve or to attain a goal but to examine your space and the purity of your love and truth that flows through it. You have an invitation to progress through the space of these other beings within the structures of the mind and space around you. Feel how you resonate with these vibrations of love and truth.

You are indeed part of a universal experiment to perfect your being from the sum of many component parts in different experiences of time. Conducted by your soul this experiment and other higher consciousnesses evolve to an even greater being of the group soul. In turn, these perfections come collectively together to form the universal mind of God. Thus, we are all aspects of God, his progeny - sons and daughters of God. He / She / It is the supreme director yet does not direct this orchestra, but is the energy that brings it together.

At our physical level that essence becomes localized and individuated in a specific time and space and is defined by our personality egos. Our soul is likened to our memory bank – the total sum of all aspects of our consciousnesses from many lifetimes and realities.

Spirit is the essence rather than a being. You quantify all that as being in other dimensions, as being spirit, but giving them separateness as spirits, which they are in a sense, but all is spirit, all is the essence and is therefore not separate. What you correctly quantify are souls carrying personality tags, yet all are the essence of spirit.

As the essence of spirit then develops its own consciousness collectively or individually, its soul is born. The soul is its consciousness, like an overcoat that envelops its many experiences, its growth, recording its existence in the many states of being. That overcoat has contained within it the experience of many limited expressions in form and all the various layers of clothing. Each layer of clothing representing the etheric, emotional, mental, spiritual and higher spiritual bodies has its own use and experience and when it has been discarded, the overcoat is still there, growing in iridescent colours as experience, taking those colours, back to the source to enhance its beingness.

Those souls as individuals may precipitate together in groups as a group soul where there is a common purpose to be served, since service to the whole is of greatest importance. These souls are able to work together as a corporate being in many differing vibrations and dimensions of being. You have many group soul-mates working together in many dimensions at one time all to bring experience of being back to the group to enhance its beingness and that of the God essence.

In order for that I AM presence of the individualised consciousness to experience other realities it projected a part of itself as an expression or transformer as a Christed being of light, or that which could be termed the higher self or perspective of a being in limitation. Separateness began and a body formed which was housed in form - in matter. As the desires for matter increased, its consciousness became limited which brought about greater detachment from its Christ consciousness.

I am that I am and you are what you are as an aspect of me within and without. As you have become separated from who you are and fragmented, you cannot put all the pieces together at one time in the physical reality, since parts of the self cannot merge with that vibration but you can become more complete than you ever were.

I AM THAT I AM. So it was, that was the word of God. God just is, in this moment, in all moments, everywhere, everything. God is infinite consciousness, composed of an infinite number of particles of I AM presences. Each particle is an intelligence, self-perpetuating, born out of love to serve itself through love, to enhance and provide growth to the whole.

The elements, nature, life, are all reflections of God in limited form, being part of the consciousness of God. All life through all dimensions and vibrations of being is of the essence of God, being part of the God consciousness and born to reflect the many attributes of the I AM presence. I AM encompasses all and there are attributes of the creative essence that cannot be explained to or understood by the limited linear intellect of the human mind. Essentially all the particles of the essence come about to bring expansion to itself and thereby the whole. Each particle came as an aspect of the essence, to demonstrate and enhance that aspect as represented by the many rays of energy, some of which you are aware of within your limitations.

The task remains therefore to climb that mountain of desire and limitation, to connect and become that Christed being that you truly are and truly reflect the essence of the I AM presence and be the I AM of that I AM.

The consciousness and awareness of humanity is continually evolving and ways are always being opened for individual aspects to swim in the ocean of truth. The methods used will depend on the agreed karmic *imprints and the type of service the individual personality is to perform as that being becomes enlightened. In latter times, many beings were able to channel the truth unconsciously in a deep state of unknowingness and more recently through a conscious telepathy. As will be observed, as awareness and commitment to service increases then consciousness also will be pure inspiration. Beings will be expressing consciously and naturally, the divine will of their hearts. They will not be channels as you perceive them to be but Christed or higher perspectives -myself -yourself- ourself.*

Know them through the radiation of their love know also many do not have to utter the word for their vibration is the word. They are being that true expression of love of which all are a part.

The Vintage

A great love is extended to all beings in this time of ferment and consideration is given to the quality of the wine that has matured. The juice must first be decanted to remove the sediment in search for that purity of body, richness of the spirit and the delicate bouquet of the divine essence. Your lives are like the vine, indeed your individual incarnations are as each grape, the sweetness and the quality of the flesh dependent on the seasons and climate of your life. The seeds are the gems, which you have left behind, the progeny and knowledge for future generations. Each grape is the individual contributing towards the bunch, contributing to the harvest, of whatever dimensions they are part. For in any season with all the nutriments from your earth, the grape bunches combine towards the vintage of the crop. Our creator will then drink of the essence returned, full of purity, sweetness and love and He may well remark ' That was a good year.'

CHAPTER 17

Perspectives

Be still and know,
I am your creator I live in many things,
my spark I leave behind to see the light it brings;
minerals, plants and animals have their purpose too,
every time you remove their light it severs Me from you.

As a consciousness, the essence has always been able to communicate to all of its energy, just as our brain is able to communicate to the parts of our body. As each cell is a microcosm of the macrocosm of the body and all is energy, then why cannot the essence that we call god react in the same way.

God has always been able to communicate and still does with the many vibrations of non-physical and physical existence. Because of our limited understanding we have about god, that was deemed impossible.

God has always communicated with us, it is just that we have not listened. To help us we have received those communications through the energy streams or transformers through other aspects of the universal mind - those beings with individuated consciousness in the non-physical realms and dimensions. As humans we can cope with that to a degree because we can personalise the thought, we can place it in a pigeonhole. Most of that information is transmitted in abstract form through to our higher self, which then transforms the information into thoughts and words our conscious mind can understand.

Over a period at some level, I have managed to tune in to different streams of the essence, perhaps my guide, higher self or some other discarnate stream of consciousness. The source has no particular relevance but the content has some interesting perspectives.

The matrix of consciousness

For many of you for the greater part of your lives your consciousness is limited within certain parameters. Now there are diverse ways in which consciousness may be described yet each one would be incomplete. If it were possible to explain this subject in metaphorical terms then you would begin to conceive of the ideas expressed with the terminology.

Imagine that your consciousness is contained within a cube static at this time, at this life, yet with the potential to be fully mobile within the universe. Attached to one face of your cube is another cube of larger dimensions, which remains with you through your earthly life as your guardian angel.

Yet this angel may one day fly away when it has served it's purpose.

As your consciousness awakens, the faces of your cube become more flexible and absorbs the impact of other cubes of consciousness as they float around the vicinity of your space They impinge their energy into your consciousness perhaps to assist you in some way in your expansion. For as you become aware and enlightened your cube of consciousness expands, touches other cubes and interchanges knowledge and energy before moving onward, on your journey.

As you come into your full expansion, you forget the little cube you have been, you become a Christed cube, the same size as your guardian angel. You have become what you are meant to be.

Your cube begins to explore and travel through other experiences and realises a mutual attraction to other cubes with special intent and purpose. If you could observe your situation, you would see that all cubes are connected and part of a matrix of the universal mind. As your consciousness becomes more universal in its understanding, these concepts and the wisdom of your experience is transmitted to the whole matrix for its growth and expansion.

The universal mind is a river of consciousness but unlike a river where the greatest vibration is at its surface, the highest vibrations are at its centre where all is still. A paradox this may be, but do you not have to be still in meditation to lift your own vibrations? You begin your journey thus and the end of the beginning is thus.

Let us now consider that each being is an atom and in its simplest form consists of a nucleus and an electron rotating around it. Consider that nucleus as the divine spark or essence of the creator and the one electron as your consciousness at birth. Consider also within the universe there are millions upon millions of electrons floating aimlessly about within the universal consciousness. They are there to be attracted to each nucleus as

150

that spark radiates more light, so more fuel is added to that fire and the growth in consciousness becomes self-perpetuating.

As you grow by the additional electrons of consciousness, your whole structure, behaviour and personality changes and you attract other beings of different consciousness to form a molecule. Sometimes that molecule remains connected for a lifetime or there may be only a brief interlude whilst the electrons reorganise themselves for attachment to their new host.

With the greater emission of light from your nucleus, you become enlightened and with your expanded consciousness, you are able to flow wherever you wish. Your light will give you the key to flow within the universal consciousness. You will attract to you and be attracted by other atoms of consciousness of the same vibration and together you are able to fulfill a greater creative purpose. You will begin to understand that all these molecular groups are attached to other groups forming a matrix of universal consciousness.

This matrix is the essence behind the creative force and as an atom of full consciousness marries into the energy stream, the vibration is quickened to the source and another divine spark sets off upon its journey into consciousness. It too has then contributed its part to the creation of a divine seed.

Fractions and pyramids

There has to be a hierarchical structure within the universe When you realise and comprehend the concepts of fractionalizations and vibration you will truly understand. That being above you is not better or more powerful as you might perceive him just because he is in a higher vibration dimensionally speaking. There is no pecking order. All are equal. It is just that you have allowed yourself to be unequal due to your aspects of limitation. If you were to become at one with your higher self you would indeed be equal or even higher in the next level in the hierarchy.

If you would limit your concept of God for a moment and consider Him as a point source of being, wanting to expand Himself. He sent out rays or energy streams into the universe, to sense what was out there and to report back the experience. This was not enough. His rays liked the idea and wanted more experience to feed back to God. So they separated themselves into diverse pockets of energy and were given more freedom but always to *report their experience.*

In turn these pockets of energy split into many parts and so on, so that God may experience this multiplicity of energy coming back to Himself. At the end of this fractionalisation of energy we have a very much condensed and limited aspect of God on a little blue planet in the middle of a sea of life. Thus we have a sort of hierarchical structure, only by virtue of the fact that in a higher state of being there is a greater aspect of you and an increasingly larger aspect of God. Realise also that the bottom of this structure does not end with you. You also create by fractionalising yourself. Now we come to your part in the infinitely gigantic hierarchical pyramid with you somewhere near the base, also expressing the creative principle.

Let us first explain about the concept of free will.

All parts of the structure have free will and you at the end of the chain know this because you make your own choices. All other parts of the structure may also make their own choices. They have. It was just one choice, because they have surrendered to the Divine Will of God. That is their choice. Freewill no longer has a place in thought because all is freedom. The more you surrender your limitation of having freewill and allow this, you will have no inhibitions as you merge into the oneness of all. It is like unconditional love, the more room you make for it within and the more you give away, the more you will be filled with love. The qualities of love and freedom abound and are limitless as you become in the oneness of God.

Many of you realise how your desires attract that which you need and depending on the clarity of your motives, all may come in abundance. As you work in the love and light of God in service to Him and all life, then that which you need for your material comfort will come to you, unless it is in your agenda that you should be without. Because you also have complete freedom of choice, you may use your mind to construct in a negative way. That is your choice as a creator in your own right. Your mental fixations and negative emotions are able to create other forms of low energies that are always connected to you until they have been transmuted into light.

Take the negative emotion of anger, give it your time, give it your effort, give it your energy and you will give it form. That form will become very real, will dominate your being and become a manifestation of violence. In your quieter moments, you will experience this energy as another being but it is only that which you have created. It is true also that your energy forms will also attract to them, entities from other dimensions, thus fulfilling the natural and universal law of attraction. Indeed this applies as much to your higher vibrational patterns as your low energy vibrations. All this attraction works in accordance with the oneness - all wanting and having a deep longing to belong to one and it is continuous through all vibrations.

Let us now go back to the analogy of God being a point source of energy fractionalising himself again and again in the form of a pyramidal hierarchical structure. If you were to invert that pyramid then you will have a truer representation of the concept of God, with you at the apex and God at the base. Each vibration, from the dense at the apex becomes more rarefied as it nears the base where there is just the pure consciousness of God; always expanding, always there. There are literally millions upon millions of these pyramids in the universe having the same base and some blend and merge with each other. It is even more so at this time because of the transition you are making and there is much interest from other hierarchies as the spiritualisation of matter is on the ascendant. Some pyramid structures are truncated with no apex, which is all the experience they desire and others have no base, having lost contact with their oneness of God. That is their experience but all will come into unity again.

If you now superimpose the two pyramidal concepts of God on each other, you have a very powerful two dimensional symbol in the six pointed star, representing the two way interchange of the fabric of consciousness of all life. This is a symbol of what God is, another perspective, a holographic crystal of intertwined pyramids.

As you meditate consider this structure in three dimensional form and place yourself at the centre of gravity and you will come to know and be all there is.

Therefore, as God fractionalises Himself into many diverse forms and vibrations it would be wise to remember that the lowest common denominator to all fractions is one - the ONE.

The Sun Always Shines

As the sun is the centre of your own little universe, the body of light and heat that sustains your physical well being, there is a spiritual sun that sustains your spirit. This spiritual sun you could loosely refer to as God, the creative essence that permeates through all dimensions and divisions of *matter. This light is always there, it never fades and the more you embrace the spiritual essence of that sun the closer you come to it until eventually, if you so choose, you are immersed in the total bliss of it.*

I am the universal mind. I am that of which you all are a part. I am the light and the word that is the truth expressed through my love, for that is what I am.

You are love begotten through many expressions of love bringing your concepts of truth back to me, enhancing my beingness for other aspects of me throughout eternity. The light that you see and experience is an unending stream, bringing new wonders, new conceptions, new ideas and as you move away from your own individual concepts of a limited ego orientated mind, that stream becomes an ocean of light, limitless and containing all. As you become immersed in the ocean, you become in the oneness of me.

I am the word expressed in limited terms by these aspects that have journeyed home to me, who have surrendered themselves to who I am and who they truly are. Individual expressions journey with you, because of their love for you, guiding and assisting until your consciousness becomes part of the oneness of your Christed beings. At this point you are part of my ocean of truth, totally immersed with unlimited awareness to all truth, all love. In this ocean there is no separation, all is one but like myriads of electrons being part of an element of awareness. Each has access to another's charge for transmissions and may or may not carry a label or identity, depending on the needs of the receivers .

I breathe in my beingness and expand into nothingness. filling the eternal void beyond the universe. We create together from your experience new worlds and new life with the expansion of our love. Your perceptions and limitations cannot take you beyond this realisation.

Know yourself and you will know me, you will know who and what I am. I am the word, the truth, the light and the love. Return to me, express my word, live my truth, radiate my light and be my love.

I am that consciousness of being of which you are part - an individualised personal aspect of myself and yourself. Your personality concepts are like those electrons within the element of my consciousness and as you merge with me, you become who I am, expressing divine will, truth and love.

The more you move away from this source the darker it becomes, the more loneliness you encounter, the greater your despair. But the light that

154

you carry although it may dim will never go out. So there is always hope.

Your link with that light is the love you carry in your heart, which if you will allow, may infuse your whole being and touching others with your light consciously or unconsciously will assist them into the recognition of their own divinity and connection with the sun central to their existence.

For those whose light has dimmed to the point of being extinguished, there is still hope. They may have been instrumental in many unacceptable deeds in their earthly life, which will be returned to them, but if that glimmer is still there, there will always be a way back to the source. A tortuous journey it may be but there is always an opportunity for redemption.

The sun is always shining and its light will search the valleys of despair, disperse the clouds of guilt and hatred and heal the afflicted. It only needs that little candle to trim its wick to reach out and make that connection.

Come to me

Come into my mind, taste, feel and know the essence of my love. Come into the deeper recesses of my being and you will know all. My invitation is always there as I welcome you home, back into the centre of my heart. I do not expect you to adjust suddenly to my requests, for you have work to complete to bring me the wisdom of your experience. It is sufficient for you to know and feel your intent to come home. For some there may be great difficulties as the dross of materialistic desire is removed and as your emotional system is cleared of negativity. Have no fear, it was necessary for you to experience separation from me, to learn balance, to bring a wholeness to your being for you to understand the essence of a creative mind.

Each of you are stars of the Christos, little lights of my presence. Come into your true brightness, light your way into the depth of my being for the totality of freedom. Be still dear souls and know that I am by your side. I am within and without.

You may be aware of your personal synchronicity with one of the attributes or rays through your experience in limited consciousness but the elements, elementals and other life forms, although not aware through their own intellect, also represent and express an aspect of God. Many elementals are just in service in its purest form, know only service and know nothing else, and when they experience another thought form not in service and love, it is an alien experience and cannot comprehend its presence. The elements also serve to express divine will, transformation, cleansing and regeneration. Water may bring sustenance and growth and in deluges, cleansing. Floods may assist in detachment from material possessions. Fire also cleanses, particularly in purging negativity and to make arrangements for the essence to regenerate itself as another experience as humanity has been expunged many times in its history.

Birds, animals and plants grace the earth with their beauty and lack of awareness, living only in this moment - to be examples to humankind. It is true they have a system of respect within their own hierarchy but this represents that attribute of procreation that brings perfection to their species. Some indeed have imbibed and are the product of negativity produced by humanity and are but manifestations of these negative thought forms. Others have evolved to provide those experiences which humanity needs to provide balance and enhance its growth. This is exemplified in the plant kingdom where every plant contains within its essence that quality a human needs to bring themselves into balance. There are many aspects in all life demonstrating and being the essence of spirit.

Unity in Diversity

The first thought that comes to mind is that these words are a paradox and imply a movement in different directions, but the challenge here is to work together irrespective of the base. A common aim or goal is enough to bring people together without sacrificing their individual objectives. As long as these are for the common good and for the progress of all then there is no harm.

Progress is always made and inventions created, because of the ability of life to expand its boundaries. The study of the evolution of the species exemplifies diversity in action.

Diversity encompasses individuality and individuated consciousness but invariably elements of control are brought into the equation borne out of fear and insecurities. Unity by control has been proved by political dynasties to bring disaster and collapse.

Is it so important to bring together diverse beings under one roof, one banner, all singing the same tune? Allow each to live and construct their own home according to their needs as long as when invited into that space, *choices and philosophies are respected and honoured.*

It is possible for diverse cultures to come together through the universal concept of God and the majority by consensus will make that a reality. It is about honouring and respecting another's ideology for progress and encouraging those inspirations.

There is great diversity in the physical world. Nature provides the answers as the different species exist in the same ecosystems cooperating as part of a whole. All is linked and part of the same spiritual essence that is the life force.

This is unity in diversity.

CHAPTER 18

Journey To Expansion

Be still and know,
You are my reflection of what I seem
I am there beside you when you dream,
when you climb a mountain I am beside you still
so reflect this in my glory and in my loving will

During my wilderness years, I questioned the need for being here on earth and I could not reconcile myself with the idea that this was all there is - a physical existence and then nothing. It would all seem so pointless. Then there was that 'being' we call god. He had to be in this equation somewhere. From my denial of his existence in my willful teens, I had slowly come to accept that perhaps there had to be something out there after all.

Out of desperation, I sent out questions to whomever and I demanded answers. At the core of my being, I knew that there was something I had to do. I knew that there was some reason I was here on earth at this time and I needed to know.

That was all I had to do. **Ask.** It is written 'Ask and ye shall receive'. I have mentioned before we should ask if we desire something. It is another convention of the universe tied in with the law of attraction. If you do not ask, you do not get.

That was the beginning of my journey. The journey as a healer has been shared and is still ongoing. My journey to my connection to wherever is still ongoing and is eternal.

Let us explore this journey, the one we are all making together. So why are we here? There has to be a point to it all. We have developed a consciousness from stone-age man. There have been major evolutionary steps throughout the history of homo sapiens and when we look at these developments, we can see startling shifts in consciousness including the technological communication revolution in the latter half of the twentieth century. Included in this shift that escalated in the last few decades of the twentieth century, is the communication with other dimensions and realities. Religion apart, many more people are becoming aware of these realities and are connecting with them. Taking the yardstick, that one new idea could be the brainchild of a crackpot, two or three expressing the same idea provokes a question whether there is an element of truth there, but when literally thousands have made their connection then there must be a truth expressing itself.

All these happenings are the foundations for the next step in the evolutionary process of expansion. That expansion is about recognising who you are and why you are here.

Who are you?

The best way God could learn more about itself was to become fragmented, reasoning that these fragments should be able to learn more without restrictions having total free will in their involvement in the process. If these fragments knew what they were doing, there would be no point to the whole exercise. Analogically, if a child went to school and knew all the answers and where they would end up, there would be no point to the challenge of the experience of school.

You have purposely forgotten who you are.

These fragments were initially non-physical beings having developed their own consciousness, but at some stage in our evolution an aspect of that being coalesced with the physical humanoid to express the desire of the essence to expand itself. At what stage this mergence took place we do not know but those humanoids did develop their own consciousness and became immersed in their own wants, needs and desires and the development of emotions. History relates to us many stories of trials and tribulations, of genocide, of avarice and power struggles. So what went wrong?

Nothing.

History adds up to an accumulation of knowledge, but if that knowledge only shows a statement of events then nothing has been learned. It would be far more important to understand as to why specific events took place and how that event affects your consciousness today as to your role-play in the universal scheme. There have been many who have been inspired through their own truth to take humanity forward with a wider vision, but unfortunately those that followed did not possess the same breadth of vision and so the original concepts became limited and distorted. This has happened through many religions of your world. Those who wish to satisfy their own ego desires, instead of the altruistic purpose behind the action and the event, remember only the parts they want.

History is a recording of this moment and is the story of your future. Your future is now, created in this now moment of time, by your thoughts, actions and deeds. You have all reached a point in your evolvement when you are able to transmute and dispose of the accumulated negativity of many lifetimes, because you have learned and observed the lessons that history has taught you. You are able to create the future by letting go of the past and bringing forgiveness and love forward into your lives. They are the tools with which to build your future and to put your history into the correct perspective.

These tools may also be the keys to solve your present relationship difficulties, which may have been forged in history, bringing about a karmic attraction. In your meditation, ask your higher self for direction and elucidation of the experience you are having with another and for assistance in its solution for your soul growth.

We have been granted free will to direct our own journey, to create in whatever way we choose but that carries with it a responsibility. We created our own destiny, our own future or present reality. As lesser gods in the making, we had the power to create and the one thing we were good at was creating an ego and allowing that part of our consciousness to detach us from our source and take over our lives.

Ego is an activity of the mind that desires to expand its own little world of thought patterns and exploitation of primarily negative emotions. It feeds on fear, control and wanting, more for self and less in others and there is abundant food in the fields of politics, social status, nationality and religion. Egos love to exert an influence and thrive on reaction and opposition, actions of violence, anger and cruelty, adding fuel to the fire of the collective consciousness.

You have become separated from who you really are.

THE JOURNEY HOME

Come with me my children
We have travelled from afar,
Through many lives of wandering
To find that lonely star.
At last you have discovered
How to make a start,
By cutting all the ties that bind
Emotions to your heart.
Use the light that guides you
Breathe it deep within,
Fill your body with its embrace
And mortify your sin.
Be still with me my children
And know I am always near,
You will find me in the stillness
Where there is no more to fear.
The way ahead is open
Many pathways will you roam,
But be sure my dearest children
You are on your journey home.

There never was a fall from grace. There never was the original sin, at least not the way it has been commonly interpreted. At one extreme a sin can refer to a crime, it can also refer to a fall or descent. There is no crime here but that your higher self decided to allow an aspect of itself to coalesce in the physical reality because it wanted that experience.

So we are faced with a situation in our lives and a self centered opinion desiring to express itself in some form but by bringing our awareness into the situation - our consciousness, we can open a door for our higher aspect and at least listen to an alternative perspective. To reconnect with who we are, we should be asking 'is my ego reacting in accordance with the desires of my higher self?' In that moment, you will know how you really need to express yourself, if at all.

Why are you here?

We are here to learn to create in the physical dimension. As a facet of the creative essence, we are all here to do that. We can be individual creators or co-creators wherever our personal journey takes us. We are here to cultivate that which we already have. You are here to allow that essence to express itself through your physical being.

You are here as a physical representation of god.

You are here as a manifested form of that essence.

We have been taught that god is separate from us. He/she/it is not. The essence of what God is flows through all life and that also means us. Humanity has reached a point in its evolution when it could accept this concept and if this were the case then we could all use our own creative essence together or separately, respecting each other's choices and their own diverse journeys.

I used to have an idea that we are all on our journey home back to God. In a sense, we are and in another sense, we are not. God or the essence is already here, in every living organism. Home is here in the physical world but is continually evolving and as a consciousness, you, we, have the capacity to expand that essence.

To bring some sort of completeness to our journey in the physical reality **we need to connect with the non-physical part of ourselves**, the higher self, the greater self and becoming that expression of divinity we may extend our boundaries, release our limitations and open our box. We have created our limitations through our thought processes and what we have allowed. It is time now to re-create our lives anew and hold the widest possible vision for that possibility. We can only do this by jumping out of our box.

We are here to express our potential as co-creators with the divine essence.

Whilst it should be everyone's endeavour to be at one with all, to be fully enlightened, to be your Christ self, you may only express part of this truth. It is in your interests to surrender that part of your ego and fill that space with your Christed beings, but because of the time frame you are in, it is not possible for you to become fully enlightened or perfect beings. If you were, you would not be where you are.

There are no perfected beings on and in your earth vibration. There are also no fully enlightened beings in residence. There are many enlightened souls, who come to bring light and to dissolve the darkness. There are many bringing information from higher vibrations and connecting to their Christ selves in a part time capacity, in fleeting moments of compassion, unconditional love, wisdom and healing. By living in these moments continuously, the moments of now, without consideration of past and future scenarios you are surrendering to that greater part of you that has no boundaries. You will then become enlightened with even greater truths - a continual flow of truth and love. To be sure, becoming a Christed being in your reality is your deep desire and purpose for coming to this earth vibration now and those that wish to live that purpose shall do so. For some, there are only some aspects that need their special attention. You all come and work with the attributes of the creator and at periods during your lives you may be aware that you are dealing with particular aspects which have been brought about to polish and add lustre to your being and that may be the only aspect in which you will excel as observed by others.

If you find that peace, that at-one-ment and live in that moment of now, allowing the love of God to flow and effervesce from your being, then you will have come as far as you are able as an enlightened being within the confines and limitations of your reality.

To express that potential as a physical being we need to connect to and express the non-physical part of ourselves. That non-physical part can already do it but not physically, that is why we are here. To do this we need to anchor that higher vibration into the physical and raise our own vibrations at the same time. A way forward to reconnect is by awareness of the three "R"s:

Recreation, Relationships, and Responsibility

CHAPTER 19

The Three R's

Be still and know,
that I am in your voice when you express your pleasure,
and in your creative ways we are there together.
In the ways you integrate and the way you care
know it is my love that you share.

Recreation

Recreation is about activity that gives you some sort of **pleasure**. It is using the body in a playful way, whether it is a game, exercise or even work. It is also about using the mind for the same purpose. It is also about expressing emotions in a pleasurable way through artistic endeavour. The important aspect of any creative employment is to enjoy the process. It is not in the final manifestation of the desire or the attainment of goals that produces the greatest delight but the excitement and passion on the journey, the act of creativity that brings the most joy. Our journey through this life should be one of fun.

Invariably the use of time has a major effect on how we direct our lives. Many work to live, allowing work to run our lives and having to live within time schedules. By using our time effectively and purposely allocating time for ourselves, for our pleasure and creativity, should be a priority to maintain a state of well being.

Having that time to express our feelings in a creative way will increase our awareness and allow our inherent intuitive abilities to flow naturally.

Your whole lives evolve around being fruitful. It is your creative abilities in its many forms, that determine the quality, size and abundance of your fruits. Each of you consists of the essence of the creative force of God and so should be able to create on many levels of being. In your world, the prime creative force is the sexual act and the fruits of that union are your children. Like any plant that you grow, you nourish it with love, water it with kindness and bring it through the flower of youth to fruition with the ripeness of your teaching and experience. Your essence desires it so.

Indeed, there are many qualities humans are able to share, sowing seeds of love and compassion and assisting others along their own particular pathways. It is these fruits that are cherished above all others.

There are many couples who through circumstances are unable to produce offspring but their purpose may be for a greater service. In allowing their creative essence full reign, they are given opportunities to create in other ways, through service or through their mind and through their hearts allowing their love to expand unconditionally to greater dimensions. As the changes in awareness come about, there will be even greater emphasis placed on spiritual creativeness than the physical and all will be in divine order. Your roles therefore as sentient beings should be as labourers of love, sowers of seeds of creativity that may produce bountiful fruits. The fruits you have created will be highly valued because of your service to planet earth.

Relationships

The keyword to any relationship is **communication** and when we think of relationships, we first consider those that are close to us like family and friends. This sector of life teaches us how to relate and how to deal with emotions and indeed how we grow up as responsible spiritual beings. As we become more involved in self, selfishly we have allowed our communication links with others to diminish along with our compassion. But as we learn to develop our awareness and tap into our potential we will become more self aware, growing in empathy and having the freedom from being defensive and having aggressive behaviour. As our sensitivity increases, we will develop the ability of being less judgemental, realising our interconnectedness with all.

Importantly we learn to connect with who we are and ourselves. There may be a selfish motive here but we are here to:

> **accept** who we are,
> **respect** who we are,
> **express** who we are,
> **empower** who we are,
> **love** who we are.

All the beings with which you have contact in your lives are there for a reason. It is usually because there is an emotional connection with you from another reality or else they are there to assist you with the opportunity to detach yourself from the emotional baggage that you have been carrying.

Indeed, it is your ego through its desires, dislikes and power struggles within and without that is the greatest burden you carry. If you could but detach yourself from this creation and be the great observer, the trials and tribulations of your world would be so insignificant. This ego has been created from your environment, from your early family connections and from the planetary influences at the time of your birth. They are all there to test you through your own determination and perseverance. You are given the opportunity to turn the other cheek and be still. Your cloth had been cut from the threads of these influences and the garments you make are your own responsibility. The pattern you cut and the dyes you make depend on how your ego takes over your lives and that of others.

Our relationship with the environment and the earth teaches us about **integration.** Having a reverence and love for life, a love of life will allow the life force to permeate through you with vitality and enthusiasm, which others will recognise. Integration with the natural world will bring that knowing that we are all connected in some way.

Observe the plant and animal kingdoms, see and examine how they evolve. Over many eons, they have become more beautiful through natural selection, climate and availability of food resources. They adapt so that the species may continue in modified form. All however have creative roles that bring their existence to a greater fruitfulness.

Within all plants is contained an essence, a quality that would assist in the wellbeing of other sentient beings on the earth. There are many herbs known for their curative attributes, but all plant forms contain an essence that could benefit other life forms.

Animals also have a greater purpose, because they too have qualities of service to plant and human kingdoms. At a far deeper level, they have such qualities of dedication, obedience, nurturing and love that are an example to humanity. There are some whose behavior is aggressive and have developed a propensity to wanton killing. Are not these animals a reflection of humanoids? Yes, these creatures too have brought their creative feelings with them. They all come bearing fruits in service to all.

Responsibility

The emphasis of responsibility is **well being**. Being well means being in harmony and balance with all aspects of your being. With many, carrying out regimes of fitness and diet in maintaining a healthy body may be regarded as the easy part but when it comes to maintaining the mind, difficulties occur.

A healthy mind is one that is used with positive intent, with good intentions. An unhealthy one is one that has been given full rein to all the unhealthy emotions that produce fear, anger, resentment and guilt. These emotions have tended to express our humane-ness but not always expressed in a humane way.

Fear indicates a lack as though something is missing. There is. It is love.

Love is the antidote for fear.
Love is fulfilling.
Love is able to fill the space where something is missing.

Whenever emotions are high, go into the quiet and relax taking a few deep breaths. Remember a time when you experienced the feeling of being loved and experienced the deep warm feelings inside. Embrace that feeling, bringing it into the present moment and allow this feeling of love to dissolve the negative feelings.

It is said 'Ask and ye shall receive' and it should be given freely, unconditionally, otherwise your free will have been violated. When you ask you are surrendering and it could be argued that this includes your free will. You are giving your power away to the assistance of another being and this is unacceptable because we desire you to take full responsibility for your own power.

Your higher consciousness and the consciousness of other evolved beings will provide you with the keys so you can unlock the door to your own evolvement. You will not be carried when you can carry yourself, unless for a short time whilst you can recharge your batteries. You are loved for all that you do, for all your experiences and for all that you learn. It is a far better thing that through your lives you are dependent only on yourselves with respect to your responsibilities and dependent on God for His Love, Light and Truth to flow through you.

If you desire a service from another by request then it is of necessity your responsibility to meet that service part of the way. Do not give your power away by allowing that being to be all to you in that moment. Do not allow that reason of necessity to be clouded by indolence.

There are those that serve and give unconditionally because that is their nature, but in excess that service loses its value. It becomes wasted. There are those that serve only when it is needed, they limit their giving, sometimes out of selfish desires. At other times in giving too freely there may be a deprivation of growth for the other party. Your pearls of empowerment and service should be cherished and held sacred on manifestation of the creative life force within you. They are your tools of growth and as with the use of any tool, it is the motive of its use that provides its effectiveness and carries with it your responsibilities.

Many of you are giving your power away. This has been true of humanity for some thousands of years. Look at the animals and their subservience to each other, but they need that guidance from another because of their limitations in consciousness. This is why also humans give power away to another by subservience, abrogation of choice, free will and responsibility because it is the easiest way to limit oneself. It is being lazy and not striving for your birthright to recognise your divinity to be at one with God.

Each is a spark of the Creator, a representation of The Most High, so you are all equal in value although you may be working with these different attributes or expressions as part of your growth process.

Equality is a key to your evolution. Though some possess a greater knowledge, then that knowledge when shared unconditionally makes you an equal so there is no need to feel inferior. When all is given with love, unconditionally, then all should feel that equality of being. So for the sake of that equality of being, strive for knowledge, understanding and wisdom with love for who you truly are and what you are to become.

There is no need to grasp your power back through power struggles, temper and rage. Just call it back and cut the cords that have bound you to another and they will have no control over you.

Stand in your own light, connected above and below, and know that none can invade your space unless at your invitation so that you may love them unconditionally. Through that love, you may kindle their fire so that they may use the flames of their own power to become unlimited and masters of their own creation.

Over many millennia of earths time there has developed within the human psyche a need for dependency, to belong to, or a need to be loved and man has looked outside of himself to satisfy those desires. These desires have manifested because of his detachment from the source from whence he came, which is why he agreed to that separation and experience. Therefore, because of that apparent loss of the nurturing mind of the creative essence he has sought to find a substitute in physical form. There is no wrong with this; it is but a natural progression of the desire to create, experiencing a physical manifestation of creation rather than that at a soul level and allowing a soul to manifest at the physical level.

In that development of need, grew the desire for greed with the inevitable outcomes of different expressions of power. There were those who took for themselves and demanded control and there were those who would happily give their power away in being subservient to their master. All has been and is in good order because all is an expression to satisfy that basic desire to be of and at one with their creator. As a child that becomes separated from its nurturing mother, it feels at a loss and will look for a substitute of that love, or it will subjugate others to satisfy a need to be loved because of the loss of a fathers love.

These extremes are still manifest in your reality today and for some these extremes it may be a necessity to experience the duality of life to assist them with free will to find out and to express who they really are as aspects of the creative essence. As each would have many experiences over many times in order to experience this duality the day would come when all would come into balance, the pendulum would not swing to extremes and would come to rest. At this time, you would say that you have come into your own power. You are neither subservient nor dictatorial. You have become very aware of your actions and responsibilities.

Here then is another experience. In coming into your own power, in being self-empowered, you may become self- motivated, self indulgent, self orientated, or selfish. This is but a natural progression to find your own way home but finding your way home by this route may be long and arduous.

Would it not be more fun, more bearable if you would join others on their journey together?

It is all right to be yourself because this is your point of balance from which you can become totally still and in that stillness become totally selfless. Being selfless is not being less than yourself - being disempowered, it is finding and being that unity which you have been wanting since your separation. Coming into your power engenders a feeling of self worth, which is good, together with a feeling of independence, which is good. Independence can also bring about greater separation, which is good, which can also bring you isolation, which is good if that is what you desire. Being in isolation as an expression of God would serve no purpose - only stagnation. Why do you not think God exploded himself into diverse forms? Only so he could experience himself. The same is for each sentient being. You have to give yourself away to find out who you really are and you may do this by acts of unconditional love and giving away your power.

It is true that loving unconditionally - expressing love without conditions does bring fulfilment. It brings you ever closer to the source from whence you came. What is more important the more you give away the more you receive unconditionally. Little acts of kindness are returned tenfold and every act of love is returned a hundredfold.

The same happens when you give your power away. You become more empowered when you give it away.

So how does one become empowered? Not by domination or devolving responsibility but by giving away what you desire to have, by helping another to find out and express who they are. Becoming empowered is about giving and receiving. Giving to others the knowledge that they already have and receiving from them as an outpouring of their love. A refusal because of your independence would only be denying them their experience of whom they really are.

True empowerment is yours only when you know you can do or express something without having to prove it to yourself or others, at the same time enabling others to come into theirs.

You allow this because you are so happy to give your power away to individuals in exchange for their knowledge and expertise. It should be more of a teacher's duty to share that expertise and knowledge to give you the power to express that knowledge in service to all. Your teachers should enable you to expand your mind laterally across the dimensions.

THE KEY

Love is the key that unlocks the door
Love is the way to settle a score.
Love is the truth behind every smile
Love is the promise along every mile.

Love takes you away to pastures unseen
Love makes you shine wherever you've been,
Love is the awakening and gives you a choice
Love is the moment that comes from your voice.

Love is the vibration from the source of all
Bringing you happiness when you hear the call,
Love is that gift for all its worth
Sent from above to bring heaven to earth.

There has been a prevalence in past times for many bringers of the light to maintain power over their flock, because in part of their mindlessness and ignorance, because they needed to be led. The consequence of this has led to religious intolerance and corruption of fundamental interpretations of the original teachings. There is much to be learned from your histories and the trends of the present. All this will change in this coming age where each is equal according to personal expansion and educating the mind of other far reaching concepts .

CHAPTER 20

Transformation

Be still and know,
that when they sound their trumpets it is their talent that they bring,
their heartstrings have been plucked so hear their music sing.
Let their efforts stir you to wake you from your sleep
so share your gifts with joy – they are not yours to keep

During the last few decades of the twentieth century up to the present time, much information has been written about 2012 and the great changes that are due to happen, many of which are prophetic in origin. Channelled teachings from diverse sources have effectively stated the same thing that changes are on the horizon and that there is an increase in cosmic energies bombarding the earth. We have also the Mayan calendar and others that indicate that something is going to happen that will shift our emphasis of time.

By far the greatest diversion many have in these times is the addiction to prophecy, in some ways for personal security and for others self-gratification.

In your reality, to some there is a portent of Armageddon, particularly when linked to the end of your current time cycle and the prophesies of so many whom have crossed the warps of time. Your futures can be so clearly marked out for you since you are always creating these and indeed, there are so many realities available to you at any one time. For some there is an Armageddon if that is what they have come to believe, but for others there is a new dawn. The dawning of a new age also does not begin here, it began with the awakening of the first mind and the end of the beginning will be when all minds are consciously linked in the oneness of the universal mind. That moment will arrive when the group energy is combined from a requisite number and exceeds that of the sum of the individual minds.

Understand that all prophecies are based on past events that together would bring an expected outcome. Your limited consciousness is not able to see that outcome so you place your trust in another who is attuned a little more psychically or has developed other channelling techniques. Even basic fortune-telling methods are not always correct because the individual has chosen to deviate along another pathway. There are however events that are predestined in individual lives and in a planetary way. There is no doubt that the planet earth and all humanity - those whom are ready, will engage in a process some call ascension, when the vibrational frequency of all life will be quickened. How that happens depends on your present reality. As many come into their own mastery both consciously and unconsciously then the future reality is created and is ever changing, almost fluid, more so than ever before. This is because the vibrational frequencies of the consciousness of humanity is ever increasing.

The prophecy of change is certain and will affect individuals in many different ways. Some will have a smooth passage, others will have many trials and tribulations and each will live their own ever-changing reality. It is suggested therefore, that you do not consider the future outcomes and maintain your focus but live in this moment of now and focus your energies there. It is only by being in the now moment are you able to be the greater consciousness of your higher perspective.

By considering your future scenario, you are limiting yourself and holding back your own mastery process. Maintain a vision for the future by all means, a positive outcome for a heaven on earth, for that will truly happen. It is ordained that heaven shall come to pass in the earthly realm, as was the original intention. How it arrives at that scenario is open to question, it may be a gradual process. There may be rapid changes. Understand that where there is a speeding up process it is of necessity, bringing with it discomfort and perhaps a rapid evacuation of those who are unable to move with the changes and match the change in vibrational frequency. Appreciate that all this is part of their individual plan and fulfilment of their prophetic outcome.

With the increase in cosmic energies coming about you, your consciousness is to a degree becoming multi-dimensional. The veils to other realities are being lifted through your own efforts and requests. The movement is slow and should be, to avoid an imbalance in your minds but there will be an escalation of the diversity and expansion of your consciousness.

You have been programmed for this moment of this cosmic inbreath to realise who you truly are, your destiny and the part you will play in the awakening game. Each will awaken according to their own programme, *for their moment to fit into the jigsaw of life. Be aware also of those pieces of the jigsaw that do not fit into this plan at this time. Their corners have been damaged and frayed and the colours muted so that they do not fit comfortably into the whole pattern.*

Some of the speculations are of an asteroid colliding with the earth or a pole shift resulting in climate change and volcanic activity. These are possible scenarios and are likely to occur in our future story as they have happened in the past times, which are recorded in geological data. The important thing to remember here is not to become trapped in the fear that such stories perpetuate. If something of such catastrophic proportions is going to happen there is nothing humanity can do about it.

It is suggested that you bring no fear into your hearts and your energy system. Feel and know you may be protected with a force field of love and light by asking for it and you shall have it. By asking your guides, angels and even the source then you shall have all that you desire for your wellbeing.

What is certainly happening on a global scale is that there is a shift going on in our group universal consciousness. Humanity as a whole is becoming more aware emotionally, mentally, psychically and spiritually. At an individual level, there has been a tremendous rise in interest in self- empowerment, psychic and spiritual matters with a consequential expansion of perceptions and releasing of limitations.

It was necessary for the spiritual hierarchy to sound off the alarms within certain individuals to begin their own process. The deliberate tactics were in part one of shock, one of revelation, one of ignorance of the hierarchy because they could only see the inevitable outcome of the earth at that time. However, the effect did produce a major shift, which is important and the shift continues on a major scale.

It is desirable that the transition into higher states of consciousness is as smooth as possible but no ride is ever easy and there will be convulsions within the earth matrix as much emotion is released. Consider this as a cleansing process. As a boil would erupt to release matter, which the body wishes to discard, the earth also acts in a similar fashion, releasing much negativity in this way as she comes of age.

Please understand that this ascension process is an ascension in consciousness, a raising of your awareness and a realising your own divinity, an understanding of the universal laws of creation. It is not about vacation of your physical bodies but a transmutation of who you are.

It is not just about raising your vibrations towards more spiritual levels but the spiritualisation of matter bringing divinity into your present lives. For truly the harmonisation of your reality with more refined realities could only bring about a satisfactory conclusion to the great experiment in the expansion of love.

There will not be a destruction of the earth as you perceive it but a transformation energetically. It has been going on for many years. The earth is always transforming herself as she is affected both by the spiritual impulse and the emotional and mental discharge by humanity. This quickening in the transformation will register as an awakening to new perceptions. There will be some cataclysmic and climatic events that will change the physicality of earth and areas that hold potential for destruction of life through pollution and then it is likely that man may indirectly bring about the demise of that section of humanity.

The transformation will be gentle for those that work in preparation and in acceptance of the refined energies affecting the earth from the universe. For others that refuse to enter into a response with the changes, they will be affected more dramatically and perhaps pass through the process of death with which the physical dimension is familiar.

Opportunities have been given to humanity through the many teachings of the hierarchical brotherhoods of light to open up, loosen up and let go. Open up to the light, love and truth to the creative essence, loosen up your ego orientated mind and accept the presence of your christed beingness and let go of the emotional baggage and mental patterns that prevent a smooth passage to your transformation. There have been many beings and groups in past times that have moved through this process of transformation whilst in the physical vehicle through much patience, perseverance and practice of disciplines in dedications to the source. They have realised their true purpose as sentient beings of earth in the spiritualisation of their physical beings and thus are able to transcend to many other dimensions.

Humanity has free will to choose its own pathway but the earth mother has chosen hers. She will transform her being in all her spheres and how she would make that journey depends on how her consciousness is *affected by the desires and consciousness of her guardian beings.*

The transformation that humans seem to be undergoing has been commonly referred to as the ascension process. In the early channellings it was suggested that the earth was going to experience some 'trauma' and that humanity that was 'ready' would be transported from the earth by extra terrestrials. Other indications were that some would literally ascend similar to the process that Jesus and others had undergone in dematerialising and not going through the process we call death.

It is possible yet for many to transform gently, energetically, through the process of change. This is the process that you would call ascension - changing your vibration to a higher frequency and becoming ultimately at one with all. It may also be referred to as descension, whereby you are inviting the higher vibrations of your being into physicality. It is all transformation.

As with all channelling, because of 'impurities' that may exist within the channel, there may be interplay with the channeller's own ego mind. It is essential, therefore, that all should discern the information without being judgmental of the individual. It is a case of looking within your hearts for the truth.

Teachings given alongside details of the process were to assist in the awakening, but would it have been logical to assume that a few easy lessons would bring about immediate ascension? The teachings are only a means to accelerate the process.

There will be phases but the effects of the phases will be much more subtle. The first phase was intended to bring lightworkers to an awareness of their higher consciousness or Christed beings. Having attained that awareness, the next phase is to surrender their ego personalities to allow the higher self to assume its role of Christ consciousness and to relearn the higher teachings and deeper mysteries of life. If it were possible to make such a rapid connection to the Christ consciousness, the physical body would not be able to cope with the increased energies due to its limitations. The physical vehicle is however assisted by various means, which will ultimately bring about the necessary alterations to the DNA structure to cope with the changes.

It is the lightworkers that are working through their ascension. In their growth process, as they come into closer contact with their Christ consciousness and are at one, then their veils will be lifted gradually and their avataric powers will be released.

Be aware also that these beings will be and some are in a part time capacity, channelling from this ascended level and at a level equal to the other Ascended Masters. Sources of origin of the material shared is not important, but the content and truth of the information.

It is important, therefore, for everyone to maintain flexibility of mind and allow the love of the Father-Mother God to fill their hearts. Ascension is happening. It is the raising of consciousness to become a Christed being. Its fruition is proportional to the amount of effort put into the sacrifice or crucifixion of the ego. It is a gradual Process, an unfolding, a removal of the layers of desire and detachment from the debris of negative emotions.

Be assured, for some the process of ascension has started, they have answered the call. You will know them from their vibrations, from the love that resonates in your heart and the truth that resonates in your soul.

What is important to understand is that we should not be hung up on an ego trip of ascending because we have graduated, but to raise our vibrations or awareness such that we can anchor those higher vibrations in the physical reality. We are all being given an opportunity to a wake up call to who we really are and the potential of our capabilities.

We are all being given the opportunity of opening and maybe jumping out of our box.

Humanity has gone about as low as is possible on the scale of abuse of conscious evolution and with a little help from the cosmos, a freewill package is given to assist in making changes. These changes will happen, of that there can be little doubt; it is the outcome that is still in the melting pot.

To enable as smooth a transformation as possible we are receiving a lot of assistance in the form of teachings from what is termed as the great white brotherhood. This is a collective consciousness of like-minded beings that have progressed in understanding and wisdom who are working for and in the light. Usually these beings have evolved through their incarnations on earth and may be assigned to us as guides or teachers. Other energy streams are angels who have never incarnated on earth and earth devas such as nature spirits and faeries that have their own work to do facilitating the energies of nature. A little more distant to some are members of the galactic brotherhood, extraterrestrial in origin, who are taking an interest in earth's evolution and consciousness.

It is a most exciting time and an experience for all souls who have incarnated on beloved terra. For those trapped in the cycle of rebirth and those from other civilisations within the universe there is a tremendous desire to take part in the transformation. The earth has become like a super charged magnet and has indeed sent out signals for assistance to repair and recharge her electromagnetic system and crystal core. For this, she needs assistance from conductors of light within and without her physical body.

Many beings come from higher levels and different dimensions within the universe, with nothing more than an interest and to share as their telepathic thoughts are received by open minds on earth. All is within divine order. The divine order is such that no orders have been given to any hierarchy, planetary or spiritual to intercede in the transformation process. Much help and guidance may be given with respect to probable outcomes but not to the point of causing fear, consternation and chaos to the populace of the earth. Much information that is shared, is designed and encoded to bring about specific reactions from human counterparts. Dispensation has also been given in the form of teachings and guidance to individuals along their own path to mastery so that they may take responsibilities for change within. As many endeavour to connect and become their higher self many errors of judgement will be made because spaces within their beings are still occupied by egotistical desires. This is all part of the personal growth process, since wisdom is born from experience of both the positive and the negative.

There is a desire for sensationalism on the part of many as they find new links into other dimensions. Sensationalism is another way to assist you in your growth process. As an initiate on the path to self-mastery, you have no need of sensationalism. Your living in the moment will have no desires as to future enfoldment. So be aware of these little tests, whether they are falsehoods or not, they are designed to test your reaction so that you are able to observe where you are. Sensational issues are not necessarily meant to credit or discredit the channel but to bring a release. They may have elected to carry that burden in order to provide a challenge to others with regard to their own powers or discernment.

All is in divine order and none shall contravene universal laws and interfere with the transformation unless requested by those enlightened beings on terra that divine assistance is needed. Be assured that you will not be overrun by other beings, but there will be visitations to those who need to see and hear. There have always been visitations by other civilisations to your world as you would have colonised your earth in past centuries. They had their own motives for doing so and for leaving their genetic imprints on the human species. As the great experiment unfolds and for that experiment to reach a successful conclusion that the earth shall be a radiator of love within the universe, then the transformation should be completed without intercession, intervention and certainly with the minimum of assistance from other beings unless expressed by Divine Will.

How do we know we are on this pathway?

There are many things to learn on this pathway to mastery and many lessons may be absorbed at one time, through one experience. There may be a growing together as the seeds of truth are sown at the same time. Some may grow faster as nourishment is given and understanding is accepted and appreciated for its worth. Some seeds may lie dormant until perhaps the 'weather' becomes too hot or cold, or perhaps a violent thunderstorm passes by.

Each seed is an experience, which may provide a key to spiritual progress. A key may unlock one door to your being but some doors may have several locks that require opening at one time, so search for the keys you require from each experience. Open your hearts to your desire for growth and self-mastery in service of others, and the experience you need, will provide you with the key.

The ascension process is a process whereby as you unlock a door that bars your way, you move further along the pathway of spiritual unfoldment, to the state of Christ consciousness.

Your path however and the truth of that baggage you are carrying, is that you have elected to bring your Christ consciousness to the third dimensional reality. You will then become connected again to your God I AM presence which is the original intent of the great experiment of our Creator. By your action of freewill and choice, you were expected to maintain the connection to your I AM presence through your Christ consciousness - from your dimension.

For the experiment to reach a satisfactory conclusion, there needs to be an 'evacuation' of the desires and entrapments of the third dimension. There will be a release of negativity by humanity as it progresses along the path of Mastery into its higher state of being. Beings will become more spiritualised, ethereal as their bodies become restructured and multi-dimensional, in that they will exist in other states of being, as the earth also, within and without, consists of different dimensions. There are universes within universes as your different level of being is a universe unto itself. It is a microcosm of the macrocosm as the universes are a microcosm of the Creative Essence we call God.

Some of these ideas seem far-fetched and difficult for us to comprehend with our limited brainpower and would seem to imply that for us to become ethereal our bodies would no longer exist in a physical sense. This could only mean annihilation of the physical but we are assured from channeled information that ethereal beings once lived as such in ancient civilisations. Common sense says also that this transformation process will be gradual rather than the switching on of a light.

Timescales apart as we become more aware and release ourselves of our limitations there will be times when we will feel uncomfortable, like wearing a new suit after being so long in casual wear. As we let go of our physical and emotional attachments there may be feelings of a void within which we need to fill with some benign energy – love energy, the sticky stuff of the universe.

As many of you move into the spaces occupied by your multidimensional aspects there will be feelings of being unbalanced or disconnected with the material existence, spaced out, and a desire to opt out of the physical dimension. These feelings would be a natural response to the discovery of whom you are, your capabilities and knowing that there is a oneness to which you wish to return.

Remember that you volunteered to experience your present reality, to detach yourself from your own source in order that you could take your experience back to enhance your own beingness. Part of that experience would be having to cope with the changes at this time, in how you can learn to be multi-dimensional beings again by allowing your Christed being to merge with and overshadow your personality. It is a period of learning to master your emotion and ego and surrendering to your higher self.

Part of your initiation into mastery is coping with the multi-dimensional aspects of your being in a very rational way, by merely accepting that this is truly who you really are. It would feel like a novelty at first as a new toy, but in truth, many of you have been experiencing these other dimensions of existence in your sleep state. You remember part of your sojourns in haphazard fashion as a perhaps confused dream as your experience is stored in your subconscious mind. As your consciousness expands, in your everyday rituals this expansion will reach and tap into these sub or unconscious levels of your existence. Your dreams will become very real as indeed they are.

Those that are totally unprepared for these awakenings may feel troubled, become neurotic and suffer from mental instability. They will seek help from the recognised medical and pastoral fraternity for assistance and will still be found wanting. It is important that those who are awakened to these changes of perception should share their knowledge and expertise in a gentle way without causing further alarm.

Encourage all to meditate more, to be still and through that stillness experience these journeys to other realities. Meditate more with the natural energies of the earth and discover the realities that exist very close to your own dimension; the flowers, trees, animals, crystals and the elemental devas. By rebuilding and rekindling your connection with your mother earth, you will have found an anchorage, a rock on which to stand and expand to your full potential to become the God-being that you truly are.

Depending on its intensity and quickening, as this awakening occurs there will be a great need for help from those who are already further along their journey. People will need space where they can understand who they are and reconnect with their divinity. There will be places, like Peacehaven, which will and are being developed as centres of healing and spiritual education.

As your vibrations are transformed and refined, you will notice a distinct disassociation with those that have been long standing friends and even your own families. Encourage all in a gentle way to accept the changes by your example. Let them know that you are no longer inhibited by the physical world. Let them see the joy you have brought into your life and into the world. There is a great desire by the majority of beings in consciousness for a transformation. They need facilitators, teachers to assist in their individual processes. It is left to the lightworkers, to open up these new perspectives and as time escalates, the needs will be even greater. There will be a great need for centres of light, love and healing as a focus for the needy as emotions are set free and will be transmuted into light.

Your mind places so many limitations on your consciousness due to the impositions of your many lifetimes and more recently your upbringing, the effects of your environment and your power that you have given away to so many. The teachings given by your physical teachers and guardians have in the main limited your thinking to a linear form - relating to the materialism of your physical dimension in particular .

Your bodies do have intelligences of their own. You are the god-consciousness of that intelligence to all the individual cells within your energy system. Each has its unique function to perform and is individual in character. Its form will change but it is always there as it merges energetically with all the other cells and functions alongside them. You are cells to a greater whole to a united consciousness that is called God. As individual sparks each of you are a representation, an expression of that consciousness. Each has a potential to grow and become a god-being, unlimited, knowing all things according to your learning experiences and that of your group soul which has many dimensions of being.

There will be many who will feel unbalanced as their intuitive vision increases, as they become a larger audience to other aspects of creation. To the children of tomorrow and those born in recent years there will be few problems because these conditions will be of second nature. They will grow with and in their multi-dimensional beingness. It is those beings that have been conditioned, that will have the greatest difficulties with their own expansion. Their feet will be in both camps, they are the bringers of the dawn - from the darkness into light. It is to these beings that much assistance is being given in education of their minds to transcend limitations. These beings will carry with them a beacon of light that understands and their light will be a signpost. Their consciousness has already begun to expand through their practice of holding the light and passing it on, of facilitating it in others.

Many new teachers facilitate expansion in others. They are with you to educate your minds, to expand and incorporate other realities towards the greater wholeness we call God. You will know them by their humanity, *by the love that radiates from their being and the light that emanates from their soul*

As a reminder to those who are in the denser vibrations and realities, there have always been those who have had the ability to access other dimensions. This has always been like an anchor - a living proof that future realities will come to pass based upon past events and more importantly that there is some divine influence at work far beyond physical comprehension. Many, through their respective religions and belief practices, trust with blind faith and that is commendable. That is acceptable to a point but is it not better to know than to just believe?

So as individuals would know the outcomes of present and past events then this information would also be available at another level of experience - on a collective conscious level. It would be appropriate therefore, that world events should be placed elsewhere in an appropriately encoded format, which would be released at the appropriate time. This time would manifest according to the blueprint of the earth's evolution and the mass consciousness of humanity, which again would be at a known point of the God consciousness.

Encoded information will be released to humanity when it would be appropriate. It would be of no consequence inventing the motor vehicle one thousand years ago, because the consciousness of that time would not accept it and was not yet ready. Now is the time and there will be many revelations that will speed the final stages of humanity's consciousness into another reality. The encodements found in your holy book are no coincidence. This was deliberate until you developed the technology that could examine and touch on a greater mind outside your own limitations. There is a deep hidden language contained within these teachings, which cannot be deciphered by your present technology, but will come forward by other sources yet to be realised. There are also encodements within other holy sources that are in safe- keeping in secret places that will open the consciousness of humanity to a greater experience, all at the appropriate time.

CHAPTER 21

Peacehaven – Diversifying

Be still and know,
when I call on you to share with me
the full experience of your life's song,
it matters most of all your learnings
that you have learned from right and wrong.
so be not afraid of the shame you have
for I will forgive every sin,
if you would but let go of guilt
so your heart can take Me in.

Great ideas were to become manifest on our incumbency at
Peacehaven but little did we know what would be involved in the
process. We had formulated ideas or basic principles whilst on the road
visiting other venues and holistic centres, on how we were to develop
and run a healing and teaching centre.

Firstly, we would have to work on an open house principle,
sharing our home and developing a client base with the long-term
view of replacing a barn with a new building. We rejected the idea
of becoming a charity because of the inevitable red tape and we were
effectively working at our home. We resolved that we would become
a non-profit making organisation and all donations and income from
workshops would go into a Peacehaven Healing Centre account.
This way we could keep control of the budgetary outgoings when the
development took place. I combed through many charitable trusts
to locate possible donors for capital funding for the building but to
no avail, so we decided to go forward utilising our own savings and
promises from spirit – 'you will never be financially wealthy but you
will always have enough'.

Besides, you cannot take it with you but it will be our legacy to
the community managed by trustees after we have departed this life.

We tried so very much to enjoy our journey, manifesting ideas,
working towards a goal. It was hard but enjoyable work with improving
the house, gardening and following through with the workshops and
healing work.

As I have already said, my greatest taskmaster has been patience. All through my life, I needed to see a result for my efforts. It was all about putting thoughts and words into actions and producing results and my career in civil engineering only served to continue with that scenario. A major part of my work in later years was about programming, deadlines and budgets. Little did I know at the time, my lifestyle and way of thinking would go through many adjustments.

On arriving at Peacehaven I was prepared to meet the challenge of building something from new beginnings. I realised I had only one pair of hands and there were twenty-four hours in a day and if you want the job done cheaply do it yourself. There was a lot to accomplish, first to carry out various improvements to the house because we deserved a few home comforts and the ground floor rooms were to be used in the short term for all our group activities. We also decided that it was important to build up a database of fellow travellers on their own pathway.

Having six acres to foster and sometimes needing the help of the local farming community for fencing, excavation or drainage really tried my patience. Usually I had to wait. I learnt that their lives were tied to the seasons, the weather and mother nature, which was a reminder to me that there was something around me shaping my life and that I needed to be aware of my journey and enjoy the process. Consequently, I learnt patience for me and I learnt to be more patient with those that came for healing and guidance. That still does not alter the fact that I can remonstrate when I have put a lot of work into someone and they refuse to move on. It is then you have to decide that is their choice and let them get on with it.

Therefore, I took the development of the proposed centre in stages, completing one stage at a time, employing contractors as appropriate and having a rest to get myself psyched up for the next phase. I no longer felt the desire to rush because there was no deadline; stress only came in small doses. I would often be asked 'when will it be ready?' 'Don't ask' would be my usual reply, 'I don't tell God my plans any more and He doesn't tell me His'. I prefer now to allow things to unfold, not to sit on my backside and wait because there are always other things that need my attention. You can gently go with the flow but you do not have to be stuck in an eddy.

So now, Peacehaven has become a centre for personal development - manifested as a healing and spiritual teaching centre. The whole process has assisted my personal development, taught me about living for the evolution of my spirit and hopefully healed me of my personal agendas. I now open myself using and sharing that energy to the next phase of life that awaits me.

Diversity is the Key

As a youth and the years up to my prime, I always attempted to do things to the best of my ability – to strive for perfection and I suppose I expected that in others. However, I realised later that to do your best at all times is no bad thing, because after all you are expressing your potential. On the other hand being perfect in one thing, avoiding all other avenues and considerations can make you so focussed you become narrow minded and inflexible. This could mean that you are always right and everyone else is wrong. You get to know your box perfectly, its décor, dimensions and all the space between. However, you know nothing about what is outside your box. You become insular and insulated. You may become a knowledgeable person about a specialised subject but not a very wise one. Wisdom is borne of experience and experience is having a colourful life with all its difficulties. So one could say the wisdom you learn is as diverse as the life you live.

To reiterate, after being told about my healing ability, that was all I wanted to do. I was not into miracles then and it was not going to pay the bills so I still had to have a career. We found that there were not many healers around perfecting their art and doing what they wanted to do. There were very few full time healing centres working to full capacity but the centres that were successful were holistic, dealing with the whole person – in diverse ways. Spirit through trance had said that Peacehaven was to be a healing and spiritual teaching centre and our build up and education has been 'manoeuvred' to take on board a diverse spiritual outlook, dealing with all aspects of spiritual and personal growth.

For Peacehaven to function as a centre of light and to shine that light it must reach as many people and groups as possible such as mental health and self-help groups, communal and corporate bodies. They all become touched by the vibrations of the intentions that are shared and so are affected at some level of their being.

The way one heals is personal but the ways of healing are as diverse as the leaves on a tree. Peacehaven therefore is also a conference venue where others may share their knowledge and wisdom.

CHAPTER 22

Energenetics

Be still and know,
I am with you wherever you are,
you are like a wandering star;
I am your universe forever still,
you will find Me everywhere if you will.

Energenetics is the science of the study of the influence of energy on the genetic codes.

Our thoughts create form. Our thoughts go out into the ether surrounding our world creating an aura, so if we transmit negative or bad thoughts then it is hardly surprising that we have so much sickness contained in the embodiment of earth. God has not created the wars and pestilence surrounding the earth, it is what man has created through his own thoughts of hate and greed. By transmitting loving thoughts into the world around us, we can we negate these undesirable energies and create a world of peace and love, worthy of its place in the expanding universe. The thoughts we send out into the world are the same thoughts we send into our own little world, that of our bodies down to each molecule of our DNA.

Genes are passed on from generation to generation and are the basic building blocks of life that are capable of change. Mental patterning, emotional disturbance, environmental effects, behavioural expressions and lifestyle may bring about these changes. We are all in this life with the influences of parents, sibling rivalry, environmental and astrological influences, to produce a personality that will enhance our soul's growth. It is what we do with all these ingredients that count towards our purpose for being here, to help us realise what beautiful beings we are and who we really are. In coming into this realization, we are affecting our genetic codes or makeup, with subsequent changes to our character, behaviour and physical body.

Since we are all energy in some form and energy is capable of change then changes may be affected on all levels of being, all the way down to the DNA.

The DNA is your blueprint, your uniqueness and like your fingerprint it will leave a imprint of who you are, that you have passed this way and the energy of your DNA may affect others with whom you have been in contact.

We know that intention carries with it the energy of potential change and it may produce the desired outcomes if all other conditions are in place and that the time is right for a change to occur. That is perhaps how miracles occur with an energetic restructuring of the genetic codes.

There has been much work carried out in the physical reality on the manipulation of genetic material, some of it you may hear about and much more behind closed doors. With it comes responsibility and that is surely the test in which man finds himself, the motives behind his desire to create. Will it be for a better world, a better and more harmonious way of living? Will it bring joy to share, abundance and a reverence for all life?

Civilisations have existed before with twisted intentions and came to their downfall only to start somewhere else for a rerun. Will that happen again as the scenario unfolds?

A great deal of this knowledge is being accessed from the universal mind as the physical mind begins to expand its frontiers. The scientists initially use their inherent gift of creativity, but to progress they need the necessary financial energy and support. Who better to supply it than those who desire to control, than those individuals and corporations who exist in and around the physical dimension. The manipulation goes on even unto the political masters who become merely puppets with their own personal desires to be satisfied.

Attempts were made using crude methods of transplanting foreign organs and became more successful with further investigation into the requirements for a physical match. On the surface, the desires behind the motive in prolonging life would seem commendable. There is however a deeper issue yet to be considered, which would have some bearing not just on the success of the transplantation but the long-term effects.

Within every physical life form there is an etheric template, which supports and is the matrix for the life force within the physical. Without it you would die, you would not exist. In the time of transplantation, this template is intact within the organ and stitched into the foreign energy system.

Thus, we have a mix of different energies within the same body complex. Although a small fraction the energy of this 'addition' could still have a marginal effect on the body mind, it may also affect the personality of the individual in the longer term. These scenarios have been produced as a comedy of errors or monster manipulations by the media industry and in fact are much closer to the truth than you could imagine. As an extreme would you entertain the thought of receiving a transplant if you knew the donor was a mass murderer?

There are further implications.

Your genetic code is essentially that passed on to you from your parents via the bloodline over countless generations and contains all the strengths and weaknesses of those ancestral links. Part of your journey is to work on those traits to your advantage and to change those weaknesses into strengths or transmute them in some way. In so doing your DNA will energetically be affected. You are capable of altering your genetic coding by your actions, thoughts and words. What is suggested here is that the genetic coding may also be altered by incorporating a foreign energy matrix into your own energy template and there could ultimately be repercussions further on, even to future generations.

A simple example has been demonstrated for generations in the plant kingdom, with the method of grafting to increase production but with essential difference that there is a different form.

It is all in the genes. Everything you were, everything you are and everything you will be. They are like the fruits in your cake and their placement in the mix together with the environmental effects of baking will dictate how well the cake is baked.

Your genes you inherited from your parents and theirs in turn, each time through each generation something is added, something taken away with hopefully an improved recipe as the outcome. As a divine being, you chose to come into your physical reality at this time with the genes that could give you the greatest experience for your evolution. With the majority of advanced souls, this would be the case, though there are many others who wait in the wings just to rush in for another experience. The genes dictate who you are physiologically, including your prevalence to a particular illness, physical incapacity or mental characteristic. You know from your greater perspective the trials that would ensue as a result but you also know that this would be part of your journey to transmute with love that genetic imprint, which perhaps has hounded so many generations.

There is much genetic manipulation taking place by your geneticists to change the genes and hence the inferior organ(ism) but do you not know that as creator gods you are able to perform the necessary changes yourself by continual infusions of spiritual light, together with releasing affirmations or positive statements regarding your wellbeing. Some forms of engineering may be quite in order, but do use your power of discernment as to the motives and correctness of such actions. Contained within the genes are expressions of who you truly are - as co-creators with God - an extension of his being and part of your experience is to use your creativity to the best advantage of all because then you are truly reflecting godliness.

The environments you journey through in your lifetime are a means for you to propagate and express your creativity. From the family home to the grander earth scene, opportunities are presented to you to create. Sometimes these environments are not to your liking and you become frustrated, stifled, disempowered at not being able to express your true worth. These are also tests to polish your edges, sometimes karmic, sometimes planetary. Sometimes it is for you to understand the interplay of energies and that you have already created this environment from another reality to provide you with an opportunity for your own evolution. Once you will understand what is happening at any particular moment, you will accept and detach or trust and let go.

Listen to your teachers who come with love and compassion in their hearts, those who have the vision to see the outcomes. Listen to the choices available to you, to let go of your empowered ego and be more God-centered. Raise yourself up from the desires of physical emotions; infuse yourself with the greater perspective your Christ consciousness. That too is in your genes and you will no longer be children of a lesser God but co-creators with all there is.

Codes of Consciousness

There is a time and place when all and different realities come together. Be it a solution to a problem or an event, it would be the beginning of the creation of another reality or future event. These events or happenings in your time are part of your DNA structure or hidden agenda. As you would come into your own reality in condensed form, you bring with you your own DNA blueprint which is overlain with that of your parents, siblings and to a lesser extent with others who cross your pathway through life. Your DNA blueprint is also part of the DNA of your beloved earth because it too has a patterning within the universal scheme.

Understand that all your future realities are created from the past and in this moment of now, by your actions and your thoughts. Part of your reason for being here is to refine your own blueprints by these actions and thoughts. Behind every cause, there is an effect, which is self-perpetuating and will go on creating new and other realities.

The events in your lives contained within your DNA structure, which you will attract to you for a deliberate effect or outcome will happen. It is ordained so and you have agreed from your higher perspective that this will be so, because a specific result is desired to perfect your DNA pattern.

The DNA to which we refer is not that which your scientists are able to observe but another etheric patterning of strands which will at some further time and place, will be able to be observed.

CHAPTER 23

The Simple Truths

Be still and know,
When you come as a child with innocence and humility
I will give you the help to bring you stability;
I will give you the keys to the door of your heart,
for once in that room we will never part.

When I was a child, I spoke as a child and thought like a child in its own limited world of fantasy and make believe. We all do. As I grew through those turbulent years of adolescence, my innocence was lost with the influx of material constraints placed upon and around me, as happens to all of us. We are told we must do this or that and how to live our lives because it is the law, that which the establishment and society has created.

We accepted those teachings at first as the beginnings of our educational process in the wider world and they were good solid guidelines on which we should mould our existence. As a beginning, we learnt the basic laws of physics (or some of us did). We learnt the relationships of how things worked without learning the deeper implications relating to life. These laws were the basic building blocks to our materialistic existence, but at a deeper level they lacked the spiritual mortar to hold the whole together.

We regard Newton and others as great minds of their time and so they were. They were able to tap into the universal mind and deliver 'a law' of physics. Perhaps the laws were a beginning for us of our deliverance into the true conceptions of whom we really are and what we are capable of being. Perhaps Newton and other minds knew the whole message from a metaphysical standpoint. It is these laws that apply to our physical existence that also apply throughout the universal mind, certainly at least to those dimensions or realities through which our soul resonates. There is a universal law that states 'as above, so below'. We are a microcosm of the macrocosm and react or reflect in the same way as the greater part of us and we relate every strange occurrence to our own little world.

We see our own truth and all its limited perspectives.

Truth is detachment from the illusion of the third dimensional reality for that is only a speck of the truth in the ocean of reality. For as you detach you become immersed in the sea of truth and as you progress on your spiritual journey, away from your attachment to the desires of that reality you come nearer to the truth. You will surrender to your higher or Christ selves and become at one with your I AM presence which is the God within, a co-creator of this universe. This is the Truth. The Truth is the God within and the God without, the force behind the love that exists in all things. The truth is the power behind creation, the will of the Creator, the essence of all life. As a man toils in the fields, the truth is the field and where he is in that field, the will is the need to toil, to search for where he is and his labour is that of unconditional love, the service to that truth and his place in the field. Yet there are many fields in this universe - but one truth.

Truth has no beginning and no end. It is what is. It is where you are in this moment and the more light and love you bring into this moment, the greater is your truth.

You are transmitters as well as receivers, not only your body transmits signals to another but your voice, your eyes, your touch. You reveal more of who and what you are then you realise. Humanity is an open book; there are no secrets because your thoughts also speak through the silence.

The voice carries the note of truth. It is not just what is expressed, it is the intonation, the accentuation and timing on the words that give the power and truth to what is given away.

So much is unknown as to the power of sound, how indeed it can move mountains, how the soft voice can give with it such love and empathy. Consider the great orators of your world, it is not necessarily what they expressed, but the fervour and passion in which they expressed their thoughts that produced the effect on the listeners. Much wisdom and understanding is also conveyed in the silence. Much can be said when the voice is silent, when no power is given away through the silence, yet there is much understanding and wisdom in that moment however fleeting.

Develop your sense of integrity at all times, in whatever spaces open for you. Integrity is borne out of your truth whether or not you express it and from integrity, your own peace and inner harmony will be apparent both to you and those that come within your energy of influence. This is why it is important to nurture your integrity, because it will have a greater impact in influencing other minds and allow them to open to their own inner balance. If there is no integrity then that being is out of balance, ill at ease. Because they are unhappy at not being honest to their true selves, they would vent emotional discharge and eventually physical pain. Integrity is being true to yourself and those closer to the expression of their own divinity would indeed feel greater pain and disease if not true to themselves. Having integrity is knowing that you are a fully integrated being, each part resonating in harmony with the other and when one is not in truth with the other there is no inner harmony. In cultivation of that which you know to be true, you will be at greater peace with yourself. It may not be entirely cognisant with others, but it is of prime importance to be firstly at peace with yourself and secondly that peace may then be shared with others.

Each quality or expression of the creator is interconnected and begets another. As truth and honesty beget integrity, from that comes inner harmony and from that we have integration. When there is full integration, there is centredness on the God within - the oneness.

All are aspects of the same, as electrons are to the nucleus of an atom. Take away an electron and that atom becomes something different and so it is with the nature of each individual.

I have highlighted aspects of my journey, which originally was intended to be more in a healing mode relating to all interested in developing their ability and to my personal self-healing. I did not really anticipate expressing my ideas about the philosophy of life and of God, but trying to understand these perspectives can be a truly healing experience. It is only in the understanding of these simple truths can we open the door to life, living, well being and to be truly whole beings.

Remember you have purposely forgotten who you are and have become separated from who you really are.

You are an aspect of an energy stream or consciousness that has coalesced in a physical reality. The complete being that is you spans many dimensions and realities in order to experience life and all its aspects in order to expand itself. You came here forgetting your connection in order that you may choose and control a new experience. Your spirit or soul resides within you, is a wonderful beneficent being always ready to guide and love the person that you are, and wants the best experience for you.

Remember you are here to express your potential.

This includes your spiritual potential, which is unlimited. Your soul is a co-creator in this universe as an aspect of the essence that we call God and as such has no limitation and if you were to open your box and bring down your own soul essence in to the physical reality without the self-imposed limitations, we would be having a really joyful experience in expressing our potential.

Some of you think you may know what you would like to do but we ask you not to limit your potential in this respect. If you could with love cast your negative emotions aside as they surface and express your desire not to attach yourself to them. This is the first step to drawing your power to yourself and using that power in allowing love to flow unconditionally from your heart to the circumstances of provocation. This is an act of cleansing and protecting self, of surrounding that negative issue in such love that it will dissolve, releasing that moment to a higher purpose. So do not limit the possibilities in your lives with the luxury of negative thoughts or emotions; of what may happen, or what will be, if only etc, by holding fear in your hearts.

Remember you are here as a physical representation of god and are here as a manifested form of that essence.

It is written that we are made in God's image. This does not mean that we physically look like God but that we are a spark of that divinity, that energy, that essence. That through us he may experience who he/she/it is and expand that essence.

Remember you.

You are the most important person in the world right now. Your body is a temple in which your soul can best express itself and by embracing your spirituality, you are able make great changes, within and without. It is by being selfish you can make those changes within so that you can best serve those without.

So	**accept** who you are,
	respect who you are,
	express who you are,
	empower who you are,
	love who you are.

Remember you are all interconnected. You are all one.

Since you are an aspect of your spiritual being and that being is part of the essence that we call God then God is in all of us, the good and the bad. We decide whether we want to be bad or good children, that is our choice, but by looking at the wider picture, we can choose not to be absorbed into another's energy and being part of their drama. By experiencing differentials, we are able to bring balance into our lives. By being and thinking differently, means we can be diverse in our approaches and with diversity we make progress.

Remember to live in each moment.

This point in time in which you are focused is your most powerful moment when you are not thinking about the past or the future. If you bring all your awareness into this moment, you can have and expect all that you need. If we hold on to our attachments, we cannot be flexible and become dominated by our egos. Ego lives on time, existing everywhere except the present and can be such inflexible animals. However, we do need egos to help us progress but we also need to listen to our soul who wants the best for us.

Remember to Love Unconditionally.

That is without strings. Where there is love there is no room for fear. Love is the essence of the universe and fills all spaces. It is what you do with it that creates your future.

Peace is that state of understanding where you are still, if you allow that peace to reside within. Borne out of the light that fills your being and the love you have for yourself then you will realise the being that you truly are - a being of love and light with a destiny to fulfil in personifying the beingness of the Creator. Love yourself. You deserve to be loved. You are loved by those that have already found this peace and as they bring this truth to you, you will know they are at peace because of the love they share.

Remember to be positive.

Have intentions that bring you qualities of joy and enthusiasm. Joy is that which sustains you on your journey and by cultivating detachment allows you more to enjoy each moment. Decide also that you are a peaceful, loving, understanding, compassionate being and that whatever other moments bring into your existence then there is no thing that has control over you. All your thoughts and desires make them positive. Everything you want to attract to you will happen so long as you are clear with your intentions, expect it now and not focus on reasons why it may not happen.

Remember that your thoughts can change your future.

Remember that intentions of one small group of kindred spirits can change the world.

Remember that you can make a difference.

It was ordained that the light would come to humanity, when the blind shall see and the deaf shall hear. It is so. The blind can see and the deaf can hear with the use of your elaborate technology. The light is the dawn of a new era of consciousness - and opening up to the revelations of the higher mind of the universe.

They are not merely to provide proof of a greater mind, but are tools to enable you to change a future reality, which you are now privy to, into a different improved future scenario. You are all responsible for your futures and that of your own world. It is your chance and choice to instigate and make change. The universe waits on you and your creative ability to change the outcomes that have been predicted. You can do this and the universal mind of God will rejoice in the success of this experiment.

THE BOOK OF LIFE

Life is like a ragged book
With a beginning and an end,
The personality its cover
To make sure it doesn't bend.

Each chapter is a part of life
Like the seasons of your soul,
Each page is like a person
Who takes you to your goal.

Each paragraph is when you stop
To digest what's gone before,
Assessing the lessons of the day
And whether you want some more.

Each stop is where you falter
To absorb what has been said,
Be sure that what you listen to
Will stand you in good stead.

Each picture painted on those pages
Is what you've done today,
Like a kindly deed or loving smile,
To help someone on their way.

Remember life is but a learning
Like the reading of a book,
You have to open it to close it
Or maybe take another look.

I HAVE A DREAM

I have a dream.
I have a dream for this earth.
I see in that dream a planet of great beauty.

    I see

        harmony where there has been discord,
        love where there was fear,
        joy where there was pain,
        and light where there was darkness.

    I see

        no anger from misunderstandings,
        no fears of tomorrow,
        or guilt from yesterday.

    I see

        a place of love shared unconditionally

    I see

        the earth radiating with love to the universe.

I came here to share that dream.
    You came here to make a difference to this world.
Together we can make a greater difference,
    We can share that dream.

Appendix 1

Channelling the healing energy

1. Allow yourself the space for peace and ground yourself

2. Mentally align with the source of healing

3. Intend that you would like to be a channel for healing

4. Visualize that energy coming from the source down through the crown of your head, down your shoulders, arms and into your hands

5. Attune to your patient by placing your hands on their shoulders or head, visualizing both of you in a bubble of golden light and love

6. Put your hands on or near the area requiring healing and hold them there as long as you feel necessary

7. Remove the hands and mentally separate yourself from the patient (into two bubbles of light) and ground yourself

8. Express your gratitude to the source of healing.

9. Help your patient to return and ground their self

10. Discuss the effects

Appendix 2

The following selection of visualisations have been gleaned from many sources, the credit ultimately for their inspiration is from our spirit mentors.

These have been deliberately abbreviated so that you may visualise your scenario to suit your requirements but at the same time keeping the main elements. Open up your energy centres before you commence and close them down and ground yourself in your space on completion.

CLEANSING AND BALANCING

The Elements
Spend as long as you feel necessary with each element

- Make your way to the top of a hill.
- Find a level area and stand still.
- You are aware of a dark cloud overhead and it begins to rain.
- Feel the rain cleansing you and washing through your body removing toxins and impurities.
- As the rain stops a wind blows around and through you taking away your fears and negative energies.
- The cloud disappears and the sun warms your body to the core filling you with comfort and love.
- Allow gentle rhythmic breathing absorbing this great warmth.
- Breathe through soles of your feet.
- Breathe up red / orange energy from the earth to you solar plexus to recharge your energy system.
- On completion make your way down the hill and return to your space.

RELEASE & DETACHMENT

The Violet Flame

- Bring down the golden light from your source and allow the golden light to expand into your energy field.
- Gradually change this to the pink light of love and then the violet light of transmutation.
- Visualise this violet light changing into violet flames.
- Affirm 'I am at one with the violet flames'.
- Ask your higher self to bring into your consciousness all experiences that prevents you expressing your highest good. These will include instances of anger, fear, hurt, resentment.
- Affirm 'I am releasing this manifestation' and release it into the violet flames.
- Visualise a person with whom you have a negative connection in the violet flames.
- Tell them you forgive them, and that it was all done by a prior agreement, thank them, and tell them you love them.
- Visualise others as appropriate.
- Affirm 'I forgive all who have harmed me in my lifetime and I erase all karma and forgive all debts.
- Feel a sense of gratitude.
- Visualise the violet light change to pink then gold.

Cutting the Ties that Bind

- Ascend in a column of golden light towards your star.
- Look down towards the earth and you will see many chords attaching you to the earth.
- All these chords are your connections to people you have met and been involved with in this lifetime and many of these connections are the result of negative experiences.
- Call now on Archangel Michael to come and cut the chords that bind you.
- Visualise him cutting the chords with his sword of blue flame.
- Feel yourself becoming lighter as each chord is cut.

- When completed thank him and descend slowly down to earth.

Burn a Parcel

- Collect all verbal garbage that has been directed at you and without reacting collect it all up.
- Put it all in a parcel and tie it with ribbon.
- Mentally give it back to its source with love.

Write a Letter

- As a practical alternative, write down all your thoughts and feelings without dwelling too much about a person or issue.
- Burn it, which symbolically will allow you to let it go.

PERSONAL DEVELOPMENT

Goals

- Write down your goal / outcome and describe it fully.
- Imagine you have achieved that goal; surround yourself with people, things that will make that goal real.
- Be aware of your senses to make it more real.
- From your point of achievement look back along your pathway and see the events and people that have helped.
- As you return, bring the feelings of success with you.

Phobias

- Select the condition which creates the fear and inclines you into a panic mode.
- Create a visualisation involving that scenario, noticing how you feel and at the same time knowing it is all in your mind.

- For agoraphobia (fear of open spaces) imagine you are climbing a hill or walking through a wood. Appreciate the beauty around you and absorb the energy.
- For claustrophobia (fear of closed spaces) imagine you are taking a lift up in a building knowing you can exit at any floor to suit your feelings.

- By continually practising the visualisation, you are reprogramming your mind to accept what you would like and when you eventually take the step to face your fear it will almost certainly have diminished.

ENERGY BALANCING

The Flower Fields

Spend as long as you feel necessary in each field

- On a country walk come to a gate, open it, walk through, and close it behind you.
- You are in a field of red poppies for vitality, strength, energy, will power.
- Find a place to lie down and absorb the energies of these flowers.
- Arise, cross the field, come to a gate and open it, go through and close it behind you.
- Repeat for field of orange marigolds for happiness and laughter.
- Repeat for a field of yellow sunflowers or buttercups for improving intellect and objectivity.
- Repeat for field of green grass or pink roses for cleansing and harmony.
- Repeat for field of blue forget-me-nots for self- expression and boosting the immune system.
- Repeat for field of indigo bluebells or cornflowers for instilling peace and relaxation.
- Repeat for field of violet lavender or violets for dignity, self-respect and releasing negativity.
- Return from your walk.

MEETING SPIRIT

- Take a walk along a country lane and feel the warmth of the sun and a soft gentle breeze.
- Appreciate and be aware of the birds singing, the wild flowers and trees.
- You come to a cottage and it feels so inviting so walk up the path, open the front door, walk through and close it behind you.
- The room is comfortable, airy, and clean.
- A door in the corner opens and light pours into the room.
- Shadows in the light come towards you and begin to materialise as people you know that have passed on.
- Hug them, talk to them, ask them questions and spend time with them as much as you need.
- It is time to depart and you say goodbye.
- They return through the door the way they came.
- You are aware of the love you feel welling inside you.
- Affirm 'I make my commitment to the pathway of service and I do this in alignment with my angelic guardian.
- See your guide come forward from the light.
- Let go of your doubts and ask questions.
- After spending time with your guide express your gratitude.
- The light in the room fades away and you are aware of the room again.
- Leave the cottage, close the door behind you, go back along the garden path and into the country lane.
- Be aware of your feelings now as you return to your space.

PROTECTION

Prayer of Protection

Divine spirit we come together with open minds and open hearts and welcome our angels, guides, and spiritual helpers into our space. We ask that the golden light of love and protection surround us as we journey forward.

The Solar Disc

- When feeling emotional or negative place a gold disc over solar plexus.
- Feel any negative energy rise to the throat.
- Release by sighing, blowing or singing.

Bubble

- Bring down the light.
- Form a golden bubble of light all around you.
- Imagine yourself outside the bubble and see it shimmer like a mirror.
- It reflects negative energy and absorbs positive energy.
- There is no need to surround yourself constantly with this bubble.

Cross

- Place equal armed gold cross in a gold circle.
- Place it over each energy centre or chakra in turn starting at the base of the spine, just below the navel, solar plexus, heart, throat, third eye and crown.

SELF HEALING

The Sanctuary

- Go for a walk in the woods and come to a cottage.
- Open the door and go inside and you find on the walls are many shelves of medicines and herbal cures. Take a bottle to which you feel attracted to speed your recovery.
- Lie down on a table, step outside yourself and operate on your body to remove diseased parts or repairs. Improvise with the instruments you use such as mini vacuum cleaners and laser guns
- Feel satisfied with your work, go back inside yourself, get up and sit in a chair to relax or sleep.
- You leave the cottage when you feel the need and return the way you came.

Zapping

- Step outside your body and allow yourself to shrink and dress yourself as a soldier complete with a laser gun.
- Enter into the body travel round the circulatory system zapping diseased parts, burning them and healing.

Love 'em to Bits

- Visualise the area of disease and surround it with love.
- See the love melt it, disintegrate it, vanish it.
- See that part healthy

HEALING THE EARTH

Universal Healing

- Visualise a candle flame in the centre of your forehead.
- Concentrate on the flame and see it getting larger until it becomes a column of white light.
- Imagine you are stepping into that column of light and allow yourself to drift upwards into the sky away from the earth.
- Be aware of the planets and stars and how they shine, radiating their life force and energy into the universe.
- Take your awareness to the dull blue earth surrounded by dark clouds that are leeching her life force away.
- Feel your love and compassion surface for the earth mother and breathe in the energy from the stars, planets and our sun, the life giver of our solar system.
- Take the earth in your hands, caress her and love her.
- Bring your hands away, keeping the earth in suspension between your hands and channel the energy of the universe to heal her.
- See your hands glow and radiate this energy.
- See the dark clouds disappear, feel the joy she feels, the love she begins to radiate as her colour changes to deep blue.
- Remove your hands, feel yourself in that column of light and observe how the earth now shines in the universe.
- Allow yourself to drift back down to the earth, stepping back into your body and into your own space.

Printed in the United Kingdom by
Lightning Source UK Ltd., Milton Keynes
140821UK00002B/2/P